Endorsements by Professionals

Dr Bindu Selot is an innovative educationist. The areas chosen by her have a great importance for parents, teachers, and counsellors and her book *Goodbye Mom and Dad, See You in the Afternoon* serves an all-round global need.

The contents of her book will give a new vision to parents of young children, a new methodology, and a new perspective, which is the need of the hour, because the sanskars and attitudes in children begin to develop right from this age group. I am sure her book will provide a radical and progressive venue to the ever evolving practices in Parenting. I wish her success for her efforts and enterprise.

Dr H. P. Rajguru,
National Awardee for Teachers
Deputy Commissioner KVS & NVS (Retd.), Bhopal

As a paediatrician, I have personally known Dr Bindu Selot for the last 17 years. She comes across as a passionate mother and a responsible professional.

Her book is a ready reckoner for young parents. It will be very successful in making a difference in the lives of children by helping the parents and giving something back to the society.

This book is a must read for adults embarking on the journey of Parenting!

Dr Arun Wadhwa
MBBS MD (Paed.)
Visiting Consultant
Max Super-Specialty Hospital, New Delhi

Goodbye Mom and Dad is the A–Z guide for parents that provides sound advice for raising children in the modern age. Dr Bindu Selot's simple, straightforward style of writing, along with her numerous practical examples as a parent and counsellor, make the content easy to understand and extremely enjoyable to read. You find yourself nodding "yes" the entire way through the book. I highly recommend this treasure trove of parenting wisdom to mothers and fathers with young children, who are looking for no-nonsense, non-technical guidance that they can immediately apply to get results.

Steven Rudolph
Director, Jiva Institute, Faridabad
Author of *Solving the Ice-Cream Dilemma*

I interacted with Dr Bindu, first as her student at ACERT in 2008, and several times later, as a parent seeking counselling. As a mother of three boys, I have always been anxious about whether I am doing the right thing, at the right time, and laying a solid foundation for bringing up balanced, confident individuals. I witnessed her optimistic, positive, fresh, and practical approach throughout the many sessions I had with her over the years and all this is well reflected in this fantastic book she has written.

In fact, I remember the first time I went to her and communicated that I was facing a problem with my oldest child and he needed counselling. She immediately corrected me, saying that I was the one who needed the counselling!

We, the parents of preschool children, face numerous challenges during this critical stage and *Goodbye Mom and Dad, See You in the Afternoon* is full of insightful, simple solutions to many of these issues. A must have for every preschool parent!

Mansie Dewan
Author of *Destination MBA: Showing You How To Get There!*
The MBA Admission Coach, New Delhi

Testimonials from Parents

Getting your guidance in time helped us in shaping our child in a better way. The small tips for healthy food in tiffin, channelizing the child's energy in the right way, rewarding him for his achievements, etc., were some of the interesting things that brought a lot of change in our child, and also helped us in understanding child psychology. We are thankful to you for first understanding us and our family situation, and then customizing your advice, specific for our kid.

Ankit Sinha

Your sessions helped me to understand that, instead of trying to change the attitude of my kid, it is *I* who has to change my attitude by not expecting the judgment of an adult from my small baby. Instead of asking *him* to be more patient, *I* have to be patient enough to listen to him and give all the time he requires. I have to be creative in feeding him and creating his interest in healthy food.

Nutan Bakshi

I incorporated your advice to curb my son's active and restless behaviour—like I got a trampoline and a punching bag for him, and started conversing with him with my eyes at his level, which really improved his concentration a lot.

Dr Manvi Srivastava

As per your suggestions, we created a scrapbook for my daughter and asked her to paste pictures related to alphabets in it. We incorporated sand play and made her write alphabets with her fingers on the sand. We made her dip her fingers in water colours and then write the alphabets on a paper with them. We made her listen to phonetic sounds on the laptop. All this helped her to relate the sounds with the alphabets and she was able to learn them quickly.

Kalpana Solanki

My experience was awesome. My child was using his aggression for destruction by throwing things. After the session, I understood that my son wanted more of my time. He used to throw things only in front of me to get my attention.

With globalization and smart kids, we actually require smart parenting to handle them, else we are gone.

Rahul Pandey

After attending your workshop on mealtime challenges, I encouraged my daughter to create her own school tiffin menu. I now pack her tiffin according to the menu and I have been observing, since the last 3 weeks, that she has been finishing her meals every day. She feels extremely happy about it.

Seema

I came to you with a bundle of worries and you helped shed each one of them in the one hour we spent together. Your sensitivity, care, and individual attention are so touching.

Gopi

I came to you when my son was going through a tough time while my husband was working overseas. Thank you for guiding me in changing my parenting style to help my child feel happier, calmer, and more secure. You are, indeed, extremely perceptive and articulate.

Ritika

Most parents are certain their children are geniuses, at some point. We, as parents, accepted the discovery that our child is gifted, with a combination of pride, excitement, and fear.

My daughter, who was our first child, is quite smart. We felt a need to meet an expert while she was barely 18 months old, as we began feeling exhausted, unnerved, and over-enthusiastic, at times wrestling with her demands of accomplishing something new each day. We have seen her trying her hands on puzzles meant for older children with much ease—enough to bring tears of joy as well as sadness.

Once we met you, parenting became much easier. You suggested engaging activities, emphasizing creation of enough challenges and excitement to match her budding skills, along with valuable parenting tips.

Shalini Kaushal

Goodbye Mom & Dad See You in the Afternoon

ONE-STOP PRESCHOOL PARENTING SOLUTIONS

DR BINDU SELOT

STERLING PAPERBACKS
An imprint of
Sterling Publishers (P) Ltd.
A-59, Okhla Industrial Area, Phase-II,
New Delhi-110020.
Tel: 26387070, 26386209; Fax: 91-11-26383788
E-mail: mail@sterlingpublishers.com
www.sterlingpublishers.com

Goodbye Mom and Dad, See You in the Afternoon
Copyright © 2014 by Dr Bindu Selot
ISBN 978 81 207 8765 0

All rights are reserved.
No part of this publication may be reproduced, stored in a retrieval system or transmitted, in any form or by any means, mechanical, photocopying, recording or otherwise, without prior written permission of the author.

Printed in India

Printed and Published by Sterling Publishers Pvt. Ltd., New Delhi-110020.

I dedicate this book to my two sons
CHIRAG and ROSHAN
who have been my mentors and guide—it was through their growth and development and meaningful interactions that I could understand what PARENTING was all about. In fact, every time they challenged my attitude and beliefs, it only helped me to widen my horizon and remove my blinkers, to see everything with an open mind.

I take this opportunity to thank God for giving me this wonderful, 24x7 job of parenting, and I love every moment of it.

Foreword

I have known Dr Bindu Selot for close to ten years now and have always heard her speak emphatically about her dream to create a widespread impact to encourage better parenting practices. I am incredibly proud of her for putting her thoughts into action—and the outcome is this heartfelt book, *Goodbye Mom and Dad, See You in the Afternoon,* from a large-hearted person.

Citing anecdotes, stories, and strategies from her own experiences as a mother, her experience as a professional, and her interactions and conversations with parents of preschoolers, Dr Bindu has poured passion into these pages to offer a road map that guides parents towards positive and happy parenting by making better and informed choices.

"Perfect parenting is a myth, good parenting is a process." True to this favourite Amiown mantra, in her own magical, humorous, and charming way, Dr Bindu talks about some of the common mistakes that parents of pre-schoolers might make and offers simple tweaks in perception, attitude, and behaviour, to nudge parents along a more joyous parenting journey.

Full of great ideas and suggestions for creating meaningful, developmentally appropriate, and fun filled bonding moments with children, this book is a must read for parents of a pre-schooler, to-be parents, and anyone entrusted with the care of preschool children.

I would highly recommend that you keep this book close to you as a ready reference, for pre-schoolers are known to keep their parents on their toes—and knees!

All the best, as you continue to discover the joys of parenting!

Sapna Chauhan
Vice Chairperson
Amiown—Amity's Preschool
Amity Center for Educational Research and Training

Acknowledgements

First of all, I want to thank you God, for giving me this wonderful opportunity of making a difference, by giving me a sense of purpose through this beautiful journey of life.

My heartfelt thanks to my Mom, Dad, and my brother, who are my constant inspiration and my greatest strength.

My sincere thanks to Dr Nirupma Agrawal, Prof. Abha Singh, and Kavita Mathur for being great guides and mentors.

I take pride in extending my deepest gratitude to Ms Sapna Chauhan, Vice Chairperson, Amiown Schools and ACERT, to have given me this wonderful opportunity of working with the two most important pillars in a child's life—the Parents and the Teachers—and a platform for contributing, in a meaningful way, to our society. I am also grateful to her for having agreed to spare her precious time to write the Foreword for this book.

My special thanks to Dr H. P. Rajguru, Dr Arun Wadhwa, Steven Rudolf, and Mansie Dewan for being kind enough for their thoughtful endorsements.

My thanks to all the parents, the Moms and Dads, who shared their concerns with me, had faith in my advice, gave it a try, and reported their feedback to me, which has been my constant motivation to work more in this field.

I extend my sincere gratitude to Mr S. K. Ghai, Managing Director, Sterling Publishers Pvt. Ltd., for believing in my proposal, handholding me in my first publishing experience, and helping me to learn as an author. A special thank you to his staff for all their efforts in the making of this book.

My special thanks to my editor, Mr Sanjiv Sarin. His keen eye for every detail and immense patience ensured an amazing final product that you are holding in your hands.

I want to specially thank Mansie Dewan and Sunita Bajoria, my invaluable friends, who were extremely supportive and great motivators, from the conception to the delivery of this book.

Last, but not the least, I extend my heartfelt thanks to my immediate family, comprising my husband Rajeev, for giving me deadlines, checking the status of the book, giving critical feedback, and creating disequilibrium in my thought process; my elder son Chirag, for always motivating me to give importance to my dreams; and my younger son Roshan, for completely accepting me, the way I am. And a special thanks, full of love, to my pet dog Maddy, who always accompanied me, night and day, when I worked on my manuscript. My family is my vertebral column and my oxygen supply for life. Thank you, God, for giving me this beautiful gift.

Preface

Dear Parents,

This book is simple to read and understand—a handbook addressing a variety of concerns of young Moms and Dads. Some out-of-the-box ideas empower you to work towards the historical day when your child says, "Goodbye Mom and Dad, see you in the afternoon," when he or she begins his or her first school.

Since times have changed, our families, too, have gone through evolution. With the changing set-up of our society, the needs of today's children are different from earlier. Children, in the present times, are hi-tech and are much smarter, because of an extremely stimulating environment. In fact, before they have mastered language skills, they have already learnt how to handle the TV remote, use an iphone and ipad, work on a laptop, and watch YouTube links for fun. Parenting these hi-tech children has become a challenging, full-time job. To perform this, we have to be very aware, practical, and well-informed. Today's parenting, therefore, has to be logic-based and not fear-based.

A lot of parents have been using "Guard *Bhaiya*" and *"Buddha Baba"* as bogeymen to scare their children and make them follow their instructions.

But this does not work for long. Recently, a parent came up to me with a question, "What should I do? My child does not listen to me and says, 'Call the *Guard Bhaiya,* call the *Buddha Baba.* I am not afraid of them.'" Therefore, I see that only logic works, not only with pre-schoolers, but with children of all age groups.

We need to take the task of parenting seriously, a task we will be carrying out till we breathe our last. The only difference would be that the challenges at each stage of development of our children will be different.

Therefore, the moment we became parents, we unknowingly registered ourselves for a study course in which we will be enrolled for life.

Personally, by virtue of being a mother of two boys, who are now teenagers, and professionally, being a Parent Counsellor with Amiown Schools—Amity's preschool chain, I can totally empathise with the anxieties and the curiosities of all of you out there, trying to figure out what is right and what is wrong.

During my 22 years of extensive interaction with children and parents, from all parts of India, on various concerns of theirs, I found that, in spite of the fact that we are aware and conscious of most matters, we unknowingly commit a lot of mistakes. This is because none of us has acquired any formal degree or training in parenting. We simply got pushed into this sacred responsibility and now we have to perform the role of being a parent for life. By the time we learn, by trial and error, and figure out what works and what doesn't, our children have grown up, and we do not have another set of children to try our new learnings on.

Here is a book for you, which can be a tool for you to become an intuitive, sensitive, and aware parent. This book is a humble effort from my side, where I have shared my experiences as a parent and also the concerns of other parents who came to me for counselling. I believe that knowledge of some of the basic facts about the early, formative years of a child may help you and your child make the journey to school a smooth one, and the first contact with a school a pleasant experience.

These days, most of the parents route their child's educational journey through a preschool and all parents want to make these years as trouble-free as possible, because the preschool years are the most important link between home, which is a warm cocoon, and a formal school.

The experiences that children gain during preschool years will impact their attitude towards education, for life.

This book is as good as a crash course and will not only help you to maximize on the preschool years of your child, but will also take care of all your anxieties and concerns related to your child during this time.

The journey of the writing of this book did not happen overnight, but it was an evolutionary one as a professional, and while going through the evolution process, I immensely benefitted from a number of books, which also contributed in my own metamorphosis into an intuitive parent.

The material for this book came from my ongoing workshops, which I tailor-make based on my research, observations, feedback from parents, and one-to-one counselling sessions.

It is with great enthusiasm that I would like to mention three books whose contents I found relevant to my thought process, which I have quoted as well. They are: *How to Maximize Your Child's Learning Ability* by Dr Lauren Bradway and Barbara Albers Hill, *Read to me:* by Bernice E. Cullinan, and *Nurturing Emotional Intelligence* by Sugandha Jain Hingad and Neera Jain.

The bibliography, at the end of the book, has two motives. The first, and the foremost, is to thank all the writers whose books I have studied and learnt from, as a parent and as a Parent Counsellor. The second purpose, of course, is to offer you a list of suggestive reads.

Best wishes for a meaningful parenting journey!

Dr Bindu Selot

Contents

	Foreword	ix
	Acknowledgements	xi
	Preface	xiii
1.	From Home to School	1
2.	Early Formative Years	10
3.	Parents as the Correct Role Models	27
4.	Mealtime Challenges	39
5.	Validate Your Child's Emotions	49
6.	Your Child's Sleep Time	60
7.	What Is the Work of Your Child—Play, Learn, Eat, or Sleep?	68
8.	Is Your TV a Babysitter?	77
9.	Understanding the Looker, Listener, and Mover in Your Child	87
10.	The A to Z of Parenting Today	96
	Bibliography	101

1

From Home to School

Your child's first experience in a preschool setting is an important first step towards a lifetime of education. Therefore, it is of utmost importance that this first transition, from the safe and secure cocoon, that is, home, to school be a very smooth, slow, and enriching experience, both for you and for your child.

Your child will now be entering a bigger social circle, where he or she will meet significant adults other than you, his or her own peer group, a complete unknown environment, maybe a new form of transport like a school bus, a new washroom, and so on. All this might make your child feel anxious and insecure, especially if he or she is exposed to all this together, at once, without previous sensitization.

Let us explore how we can make this journey a smooth one, so that your child feels confident, safe, and secure in this new circle, which will continue to increase all the time.

Here are some tried and tested strategies:

1. Make sure that you do not make other changes in the life of your child, like changing your maid, taking up a new job by the mother who was a stay-at-home Mom earlier, or changing your current job, if you can, because these changes will be challenging and your anxieties might get passed on to your child. Children respond well to one transition at a time. If we start making a lot of changes at one go, the child starts feeling very insecure and anxious and could also become emotionally unsettled, which might prolong the settling process at school.

2. Start introducing the word "school" in your conversations. A great start could be something like this, "We have a lovely and joyous event coming up for you—soon you will be starting school!" You can then talk about your experiences when you were a child. This could be initiated by saying, "Do you know dear, when papa was a child like you, he also went to a school. And do you know what? He had loads and loads of fun, he made great friends, did a lot of exciting things, and loved his teacher." You can also construct a story around the cartoon character your child enjoys watching the most. It could also be an animal or any other character that your child relates to.

   There are many books in the market and you can use them for reinforcing the concept of starting school. The base line is, do not shy away from talking about school. Your children might have many questions, which they may otherwise not ask you. This exercise will help you to give a platform to your child to talk about his or her concerns relating to school.

> *Make sure you are excited, enthusiastic, and positive when you talk about school to your child.*

As parents, always remember that children in this age group try to see their growing world through your eyes, so make sure you are excited, enthusiastic, and positive when you talk about school to your child. Tell your child that teachers at school are very caring and loving, that he or she will get to make great friends, and friends are fun to be with. Say that there will be interesting activities at school throughout the day. By having this kind of a conversation, you'll be programming the mind of your child in a positive manner and he or she will look forward excitedly to begin school.

3. Involve your child in purchasing a lunch box, school bag, water bottle, and so on. Let your child choose these items. Once you have involved the child in purchasing them, it is more likely that he or she will relate to them and be more comfortable at school.

4. Visit the school, together with your child. If allowed, take photographs, prepare a portfolio of what all might happen at school, and talk about it daily. To help your child get familiar with the school, you can also get connected to the Facebook page or the website of the school. This will become a virtual tool for your child to relate to the school.

5. Let your child choose a small toy from home to carry to school. These objects, which are called transition objects, help in a child's smooth transition. The child feels safe with this toy, since it is an object from home and it gives a sense of security.

6. Tell your child in advance what to expect in school. While taking the child through his or her daily routine, keep talking as to what all might happen and how the day will progress in school. You may take the schedule of a typical day in school from the teacher and discuss and talk about it with your child.

7. Tell your child who his or her teacher will be. Start talking about the teacher in a positive manner. Say that she will be loving, caring, and that the child will have a lot of fun and a great time at school with the teachers and friends.

8. Arrange for "play dates". If you can find out who the other children in the class of your child will be, then you can work on arranging play dates with these children. This helps

in socializing and settling in the school. Because of known friends and familiar faces, the child starts feeling secure even in the new environment.

9. A night before the first day, avoid saying things like, "I hope you will not cry tomorrow when I leave you—mummy will come back soon." If you do this, unknowingly you are programming your child to cry by giving too much attention and importance to the act of crying. Also, remember not to get too upset if your child cries at school—it is normal for children to cry initially, for a few days.

   Please do not get tempted to promise a treat to your child if he or she does not cry and do not indulge in bribing your child with material things. If you do this, you are sowing the seeds of condition based parenting or bribe based behaviour management, which may not work in the long run. Instead, validate the emotion of your child. Tell him or her that it is acceptable to cry for a little while and that you can relate to what he or she is going through.

10. Above all, do not be anxious yourself. Most of the time your anxieties get passed to the children, because about 93 per cent of communication happens through body language and only 7 per cent through words.

11. Do not prolong your goodbyes. Let your goodbye be short and firm, with an assurance

that you'll be there to pick him or her up after the school gets over.

12. Make sure your child is well rested the day before beginning school. Children who have had an uninterrupted sleep for 10–12 hours are more cheerful, relaxed, and much better prepared for the day.

13. Do not force-feed your child milk or other eatables in the morning, because this act of yours will only add to the already present separation anxiety, which will make it difficult to begin school on a smooth note. Often, when parents force these foods, the children throw up during the day and then they start feeling very uncomfortable.

14. Pick up your child immediately, as soon as the school gets over, at least for the first week and do not be late. This will help him or her to be convinced that you will be there and not feel anxious and insecure. Rather, this act of yours will strengthen the feeling of trust and bonding between you and your child.

15. Never ever disappear without saying a proper goodbye and informing the child that you will return to pick him or her up. This is because the process of separation and return is not completely programmed and the child will continue being anxious. His or her settling might get disrupted, because of the insecurity of being left alone, in a new environment.

From Home to School

Given below are some of my experiences as a Parent Counsellor:

Case 1

Once a mother came with a concern that her daughter, Devyani, who was 3 years and 3 months old, could not settle down, even after six months of starting preschool. She said she did not know what to do.

On detailed interaction, I found that the mother did not have trust and faith in the teachers, the new environment, and the other adults in the school. She would often talk about this and discuss it with family and friends when the child was around. This was not deliberate and the mother did this unknowingly, without appreciating its impact.

We worked together on this case. The moment the mother stopped being anxious and started feeling positive about the school where her child was admitted, the child happily settled down and started looking forward to going to school and enjoying her day there.

> *Never ever disappear without saying a proper goodbye and informing the child that you will return to pick him or her up.*

Case 2

Aman was 3 years and 3 months old. He was otherwise a happy child and had settled well in his preschool. But even after 2 months in school, he would refuse to leave his bag and bottle in the cubicle and would roam around with them, everywhere.

I sensed that the child was still in a transition mode and was exploring. He was still insecure about his environment. While discussing with the mother, I advised her to send some transition object to school that the child related to.

Shortly, the child started taking his favourite stuffed toy to preschool. He would cling to this and slowly started keeping his bag in his cubicle as he gained more trust and faith in the new environment. This could only be achieved because we did not push him towards a hurried settling process, according to our perceptions and expectations. Instead, we respected the child's concerns and, as caring adults, we only tried to facilitate the whole process.

Case 3

There was a case of Raksha, who was a 2 years and 9 months old girl, admitted in a preschool. After two or three days of starting school, she would just cling to her mother and refuse to go to her class.

During my meeting with the parents, I came to know that the mother was working in an office and would always leave home for office without saying a proper goodbye, thinking that the child would start crying. This behaviour of the mother was repeated when she came to drop the child to school—she would slip away when the child got busy.

After counselling, the mother started saying goodbye even if the child cried. Sometimes she asked the father to take the child to school. There was a marked change in the child within a span of 15 days. Within a month, the child had settled well and would smilingly say goodbye to her mother.

Case 4

Ashish was 2 years 3 months old. He did not want to go to school. Every morning there was a power struggle between the parent and the child.

During interaction, I found that the family had come to Gurgaon from Bangalore just a month ago. The mother had taken up a job. To add to the woes of the child, the previous maid had left and the child had to start school as well. With so many changes, it was almost impossible for him to handle them. He could not express his problems, because children in preschool do not have enough language skills.

After interventional counselling, the mother started empathizing with the child, became more patient, took leave for six months, ensured peer group interaction of the child, and also patiently gave more time to him to adjust to all the changes. Within three months the child started enjoying school, like everyone else.

2

Early Formative Years

It was only when I took leave from my job for my second son did I realize what all can be done in the early formative years, on which the foundation of the lifelong learning is based. My curiosity to know more and more about these years started increasing with each passing year.

The most formative period of your child's life is from 0–8 years of age. But the most important are the preschool years, that is, from 0–4 years, because 50 per cent of the ability to learn is developed in the first four years and the balance develops during the rest of the years, till about eight years.

During the first 50 per cent of the development, the brain connections, that is, the learning pathways, get developed. Have you ever wondered why children do not want to do the same puzzle or play with the same toy again and again? This is because of the simple reason that the brain connections which had to form due to that experience have formed and children cannot go on repeating actions on the same connections. Instead, children want new exposure, new interactions, and new tools to make more connections.

> *During the first 50 per cent of the development, the brain connections, that is, the learning pathways, get developed.*

However, there will also be times when a child gets attached to a particular toy or an object and remains engaged with it endlessly. This could be because he or she is still mastering some skills to strengthen the neuron connections or because the object soothes and comforts, providing a sense of security. When your child clings to such a toy or object, you should let him or her interact with it. You should try to wean away very gradually.

Let us try to visualize what the inside of the brain looks like when the child is born. The brain of a child is just like the dark night sky with stars shining. Can you even think of counting these stars? There are so many of them! Similar is the situation of the brain. There are uncountable brain cells or neurons, which need to be connected to one another, and the connections will only happen with the right kind of stimulation and exposure. These connections form the learning pathways. It is from these learning pathways that everything else will arise in the future. The more the wiring, the more the connections; the more the connections, the more the capacity for learning later on.

Unfortunately, those neurons which are not used will get discarded by the time the child reaches ten years of age. So parents need to recognize the importance of these early, formative years and how to make the most of them. By investing your time during these formative years by designing your home environment to ensure maximum brain connections, you are ensuring a great input which, in turn, will give you great output, which you'll get to see in the academic and co-curricular performance of your child.

However, if you miss out on this great investment opportunity, when your child is older, the output in terms of academic performance may not be the one that you dreamed or desired. Then, if you try and increase your input by investing your full time or by taking support of tutors, bribing your child through rewards to get good grades, or trying to use fear psychosis, in spite of your large input, the output would be very little. This is because the right time has passed and all these efforts of yours may not be enough to ensure an increased output.

Children need much more than just food to develop. They need a lot of intellectual, emotional, physical, social, and language stimulation. This means they need a well-designed environment, which cannot be ensured entirely by the school. The parents have a major role to play, because 80 per cent of the time the children remain at home and only 20 per cent of their time is spent in school.

Early Formative Years

Almost all of us have heard the term "nature and nurture", that is, genes and environment. I have personally experienced this by being a witness to how both these factors influence the growth of the child. The debate is still on about which of the two has a greater share, that is, their percentage contribution in the overall development of a child. I believe that the amount is 40 per cent nature or genes and 60 per cent nurture or environment.

To sum up, both environmental and biological factors affect the brain development and behaviour during the most crucial phase of development, that is, 0–8 years.

Till a few years ago, the importance of early formative years was not recognized in India. But today, this concern is well acknowledged. Earlier, the family set-ups were different. There were often more than two children per couple and joint family arrangements were more prevalent. Fewer mothers were working. So the learning in children during the early formative years was maximized, to some extent by chance rather than design.

But if you love your child, if you care for your child and if you want to give the best to your child, then, as parents, you have to invest your time and energy in the most formative years of your child's life. If you do this, everything else, later in their life, will become smoother.

The first four years of your child's life are the most absorbent phase of his or her life. At this time your child is just like a sponge and will absorb all the learning that comes along. But does the sponge have the capability of deciding which liquid is good and which liquid is bad? No. Similarly, your children, in their early formative years, have yet not developed the ability to understand what they need to absorb and what they need not absorb. The next question is, who will decide and monitor the process of absorption? The answer is, you, the parents and the teachers—the two great significant adults, the pillars of the child's life.

We, the parents, need to make sure that the information that our children are getting exposed to is nutritious enough for their physical, mental, and emotional health—in a nutshell, their healthy holistic development. With this revelation now, parents, it is you who have to decide as to how you'll be designing and monitoring the environment to which your children are getting exposed to.

The next most important factor is that subconscious learning is the most enhanced in these years. So any exposure or experience, good or bad, will remain in the subconscious mind of your child throughout his or her life and this will play an important role in moulding the personality of your child for life.

Recent researches on infant development have determined that reading to babies, talking to them in complete sentences, and singing with them are the three most significant interactions adults do to stimulate their brains.

The other important matter is to keep the communication channels open with your children.

Early Formative Years

Many parents have come to me, saying that their child does not answer or is not interested in talking to them. I asked the children why they behaved as if they were hardly hearing what their Mom and Dad said. The children said that their Moms and Dads asked them the same questions, day in and day out. It was very boring.

When these parents understood the situation, some of them were ready to modify their own behaviour.

> *Your children, in their early formative years, have yet not developed the ability to understand what they need to absorb and what they need not absorb.*

The result was that there were marked changes to be seen. Instead of asking the same, routine questions, the parents started taking interest in what their child wanted to talk about and then, slowly and gradually, they also started getting the answers to their questions.

Do we, as adults, like it when someone at home asks the same questions daily? We can all confess how angry we get in such situations. There are wives who ask their husbands every day—how was the office that day, did you eat your lunch on time, etc., and the husbands respond by saying, "Give me a break please, do not irritate me." Similar responses were reported by the wives when their husbands asked repetitive questions about their meetings, boss, or colleagues. They also wanted a break from these monotonous questions. So too, with children. They are developing at a rapid pace and they don't want to operate on the same neuron connections again and again.

The other day, I was talking to my teenage son, when he had something important to share with me. I was working on the laptop at the same time. He lost interest in the conversation and was ready to withdraw. He said, "I think you are busy, I will talk to you later." I realized my error and immediately got back on track before I lost the communication. I shut down my laptop and got completely involved. I had eye contact with my child and listened empathetically. We got so much engrossed in the conversation that we lost track of time. Before we realized, it was almost midnight.

Had I continued with my work on the laptop, I would have lost a meaningful opportunity of keeping my communication channels open with my son which, thankfully, have remained open even today.

Mentioned below are some tried and tested strategies for ensuring maximum connections of neurons—thereby creating maximum learning pathways—and also to keep communication channels open with your child:

1. Talk to your child as much as you can about any and everything in the environment. Be sure you talk in full sentences and do not use baby language. Whenever you are talking to your child, make sure you have eye contact. For that, you should either get

down to the level of the child or bring the child to your level by putting him or her on a higher platform.

Once your children start school, do not be in a rush to throw a volley of questions about what happened in school as soon as they return. Children hate repetition in their routine—they want novelty.

Consider this example. Suppose your child comes back home from school and looks quite excited and starts saying, "Mamma today, while I was coming home, I saw two big ants pushing a sugar crystal." If you say, "OK, OK, but tell me how was your day at school, did you finish your tiffin?" The child will become quiet and will not be interested in talking to you any more. You would have blocked the communication channel for life.

To make sure that your communication channel remains open, listen as much and as often as possible. Strike a conversation with your child by asking open ended questions like, "OK, what else did you observe, were there three ants or were there two? Were both ants of the same size or was one bigger than the other? How were they moving the sugar crystal?"

2. Listen to your children empathetically. Give 100 per cent attention to them when they are talking. Try to understand things from

their point of view. This means not trying to multitask, but just focussing on listening to your child. Do not try to take a phone call, do not try to check your mail and talk to the child at the same time. It does not work that way at all. Instead, only listen and be completely involved. Do not be judgmental, do not give solutions, do not label. Just listen. Remember, if you can practice this and listen to your children now, in their early formative years, your children will listen to you even when they are grown up.

3. Read to your children daily. It could be anything, but stories is what they relate to most and that also animal stories in pictorial form where 70 per cent of the page is occupied by pictures and only 30 per cent is written text. Research says that children relate a lot to animals and hence stories around them really help them remain interested and enjoy reading.

Have a DEAR time fixed for your home, which may just be as little as ten minutes daily. DEAR stands for Drop Everything And Read. I regularly practiced DEAR time when my children were growing up.

When I say reading, it is not just reading text, but pictorial reading or picture reading. Children enjoy this and it is the foundation of all the learning they will do in later years. By practicing this daily, children start loving books and develop fondness and pleasant feelings towards them, which helps them later in their life, when they actually have to study. Because there is no shortcut to success, we have to prepare our children for reading and writing with patience and effort.

> *Do not be judgmental, do not give solutions, do not label. Just listen.*

4. Involve your children in daily household chores so that they feel responsible, get attention, have a feeling of contributing to the family, and, above all, their energies get channelized and they get an opportunity to interact with the environment.

5. Make sure of taking your child for playing outdoors on a daily basis. The duration could be anywhere from two to three hours, where the child should not only be sitting on the swings, but should be encouraged to perform a variety of movements like climbing the jungle gym, climbing stairs, sliding, running, cycling, and so on. At the same time, do not forget to encourage peer group interaction with other children. The outdoor activities are essential for healthy development of motor skills. Playing in any form contributes to the overall development of the child.

6. Expose your child to new experiences, new activities, new toys, and new environment. This will be instrumental in helping the child to make new connections of neurons every day.

7. Another aspect to be kept in mind is designing of an individual corner for your child, with a lot of material to play with. This material could be writing tools, different kinds of paper, puzzles, and books. Ensure that everything is kept at the child's level so that he or she can easily access it.

8. Above all, be a good role model. As parents, do not worry that your children are not listening to you, but worry that they are watching and observing you all the time. Therefore, first you need to practice what you are preaching, that is, walk your own talk.

9. In a bid to protect your child, do not go overboard. This means that you should not be so protective that you land up scaring your child. Let children learn through their own experiences and mistakes.

10. Help your child become a decision-maker by allowing him or her to take small decisions. Practice autonomy—with this, you are making your child independent.

11. Make your home child friendly. Remove your crystals, glassware, and other easily breakable items so that you use minimum don'ts with your child.

12. Never talk negatively about school or criticize your child's teacher. Children absorb everything and that too, subconsciously.

13. When your child comes up with, "I don't want to go to school," do not say something like, "No, you must. Look at your brother, he readily goes to school," or "Look at X, Y, Z—everyone goes to school." Rather than that, validate your child's emotions by accepting the feelings behind the concern and ask more open ended questions. For example, you could say, "OK, accepted you don't want to go to school, but would you like to share with me why you don't want to go to school? Don't you enjoy with your friends in school?" In this manner, the child feels safe to express his or her feelings freely. Then address the concern, discuss it with the teachers, but do not push the child. Involve yourself. Let the child see that you value how he or she feels and you are taking action to resolve the situation.

14. Never ever blackmail or bribe your child for anything. Nothing is more important and precious than inculcating the right values. Otherwise, sooner or later, your conditioned based parenting will motivate your child to practice the same on you and then it will become very challenging for you to handle the situation.

15. If you truly love your child, give the best gift you can to your child—the gift of high self-esteem and unconditional love. Believe me, with this, everything else will get taken care of.

Given below are some of my experiences as a counsellor:

Case 1

There was a case of Devank, who was 3 years old and had speech concerns. He had not started speaking clearly in full sentences. Obviously, the mother was worried.

During the initial discussion, I found that during the pregnancy and after the child was born, the mother's emotional health had been weak, in the sense that she was not happy with her life. She confessed that she hardly spoke to the child in words or sentences. She did this unknowingly, because she felt there was no need to act otherwise. She would reply to the child only if he spoke first. This resulted in the child's delayed speech, because the environment at home was not stimulating enough. Since he was the first child in the family, there was hardly any interaction with children of similar age group at home. There were four adults, who remained busy in their own lives and did not converse much amongst themselves, what to talk of the child.

After counselling, the mother made an effort and started talking to the child. The other adults also, together, created a language-rich environment. Slowly things started becoming better and the child started speaking properly within six months.

Early Formative Years

Case: 2

Some time ago, Jyotika's mother came to me. She said that her child did not listen to the teacher, could not relate to her peer group, remained indifferent, and was often aggressive.

Jyotika was a 3 year and 8 months old child at that time, going to a preschool. On detailed evaluation, I found that the child, till then, had no interaction with children of her age. She was with adults all the time. Whenever the child wanted her mother's attention, the mother would invariably be busy with other chores and would ask the maid to take care of her.

> *If you truly love your child, give the best gift you can to your child—the gift of high self-esteem and unconditional love.*

After a discussion, we were in a position to find a solution. The mother started being more available to her child. When the child needed her, she would go down to her child's level, literally, that is, actually kneel down, listen, and maintain eye contact. This made all the difference. Within 15 days, the teachers could observe a sea change in the child. The child became happier, started listening to adults because adults at home were listening to her now. Children are great imitators and parents are their best role models.

Case 3

This is the case of a child named Rishabh, who was 4 years old. His parents came to me saying that their child was hitting and pushing other children in the class. He did not sit in one place in the class and moved about.

On in-depth study, I found that the child, after school, was sleeping for two hours. After getting up, he would watch TV for another two hours. He would not go for any outdoor activity.

I advised the parents to completely do away with the sleep in the afternoon and replace TV time with outdoor play time. The parents willingly accepted and implemented this change.

Within a month, the child became more focused because now his energy was being channelized. Also, the need for exercise and movement of the bigger muscles was being fulfilled, so even the hitting and the pushing instances reduced. The parents also started reducing their own TV viewing so that the child could get better role models to emulate from.

Case 4

Riya, a 2 year and 3 months old child, took an extremely long time to settle at her preschool. She would cry on the very mention of school and would refuse to go to school.

On counselling the parents, I found that since the child was not a good eater, and the significant adults, unknowingly, had been practicing the fear philosophy by saying, "Chalo jaldi khalo, nahi to Guard Bhaiya aa jayega aur tumko le jayega" (come on, eat quickly, otherwise the Guard will come and take you away). No wonder, Riya would refuse to go to school, because

Early Formative Years 25

she would see many Guard Bhaiyas there and would fear that they would take her away. But she could not express her fear and talk about it, because her language and expression skills were still developing.

It was only when the adults stopped practicing fear based parenting at home could the child start feeling OK to go to school. This entire process took about six months.

Case 5

A mother was worried that her 16 year old daughter could not take decisions. She always wanted her mother to decide what dress to wear, how much to eat, whom to make friends with, and so on. She could not take even the smallest decisions.

After a detailed talk with the mother, I found that she did not allow her daughter to eat on her own, serve her own food, choose her own dress, and always told her, "Come, let me do it for you because you do not know." Even when the child attempted to take independent decisions, her mother was judgmental and always corrected her decisions. This was practised by the mother when her daughter was in the early formative years of development due to which the daughter became totally dependent on her mother for all her decisions. This became a problem for the mother, because now she wanted her daughter to become completely independent. This was not possible suddenly.

It is very important to allow your children to take their independent decisions from the early formative years of their lives. In this case it took us about a year before this teenager, slowly and gradually, started taking minor decisions and those also when the mother started accepting her decisions, whether they were right or wrong. Hopefully, this child will evolve into a wise decision-maker in days to come.

3

Parents as the Correct Role Models

Parenting is all about leading from the front and not pushing from the back. As parents, you will be amazed to hear that most of the children, starting from the preschool to postgraduate levels, consider their mothers and fathers as their role models. The rest of the children either did not have role models, or the parents did not have enough time for their children to become their role models. I realized this fact when dealing with children from preschool to postgraduate levels.

With the joint family of earlier times breaking down to nuclear set-ups, children are left with only two significant adults in their homes—their mother and father. This is a very difficult situation for parents, because they have to handle all their personal and professional responsibilities by themselves. And since we have usually been pushed into the task of parenting, pushing is something that we have been conditioned to. Parents, remember that your children are going to forget about most of the things you did for them when they are growing up, but they will always remember one thing, that is, how you made them feel.

Being the correct role model means practicing what you preach and letting your children see that you also do whatever you ask them to do. If you want your children to respect you, you need to respect your elders, you also need to respect the people in the environment, and you need to respect the child as well. If you do that, the child will start imitating you and, therefore, respecting you and others.

Parents should remember that children are not their property! Children are from you, but they are not you (Khalil Gibran). They have a mind of their own, they are unique, with their own individual traits. They just need the right kind of stimulating environment, with the right kind of role models to emulate from. And the first and most important environment is home, other than school. Therefore, the most impactful role models are the parents.

Mentioned below are some strategies for you to practice to become correct role models:

1. Walk the talk: Whatever you say or preach, you should practice it. If you say "no" to your child for uncontrolled TV viewing, you cannot watch uncontrolled TV yourself. You must restrain yourself and make your own TV viewing schedule and follow it.
2. If you want your children to be fluent in spoken English, do not criticize or rebuke them for speaking in the local language. Even

if your child speaks in the local language, you should take the lead and, in a very subtle manner, reply in English. If your child still continues in the local language, do not get perturbed.

> *Walk the talk: Whatever you say or preach, you should practice it.*

Have patience, keep conversing in English, and you'll not even realize when your child, one day, unknowingly, switches over to English.

3. Parents, if you want your child to be a voracious reader, it is not going to happen by lecturing. Read out to your child every day and a day will come when he or she will want to lead and read out to you.

When both my sons were growing up, no matter what, I would always read to them every day before they went to sleep. I finally reached my dream destination when there was a tussle between the three of us as to who would read a new book first and we had to toss a coin to decide.

4. Children learn to socialize when they see their parents socializing. So when you go to the park along with your child, don't expect your child to take the initiative of approaching another child of his or her age group and make friends. You should take the initiative, approach the parent of the

child, and initiate conversation. In such a situation, it is more likely that your child will want to imitate you.

5. If you want your children to eat healthy and nutritious food, you do not need to run behind them or bribe them, but simply act in that way, that is, opt for healthy and nutritious food yourself—though it is OK to have junk food sometimes. You'll be surprised to see how your child is inclined to eat what you tend to eat.

6. To help your child develop a love for learning, you, as a parent, must practice respecting the school, the teachers, and the education and learning process. You should be passionate about learning and studies. Talk about your experiences at school, enthusiastically, and how much you enjoyed the process of learning. When children see their parents respecting the process of their learning and respecting policies, systems, and teachers, they feel motivated. When they see their parents' involvement in the process of the education of their child by participating in all required activities at school like attending functions, parents-teachers meetings, etc., they feel encouraged. They, too, start valuing their education process and are enthusiastic about their school and their studies.

7. As parents, my husband and I have always consciously tried to be the correct role models. My husband has been very sensitive

to the need of saving natural resources, which are on the verge of exhaustion and, therefore, always switched off fans and lights when not required. We always took this initiative whenever we saw water or electricity getting wasted. All this was happening when the children were growing up. Today, as proud parents, we can say that both our sons have become very sensitive to the cause of saving natural resources. Without any pushing or lecturing, they have become role models themselves. They are very particular about switching off fans, lights, and taps wherever they see these resources getting wasted. Parents need to value the natural resources and they will not even realize when their children start taking the lead themselves.

8. If you want your children to share, you have to lead by example. It is only through your acts of unconditional sharing that your children will learn the joy of sharing. I would like to share my own experience. On the birthdays of my children, I would take biscuits and give them to some underprivileged people. I would distribute food and grains to all the people who worked for us. I involved the children in the entire process and they distributed these things themselves.

One day my son narrated how he and his friends contributed portions of their pocket money to buy gifts for a friend who was an orphan and stayed in an ashram and how they all enjoyed the fete at their school together.

Parents, give this wonderful opportunity to your children to participate in the process of sharing by wholeheartedly joining in this beautiful act. You will not have to wait to see your child transform into a person who will readily share with others.

9. If you want your children to value money, you have to be careful and not reckless or impulsive in spending money. I remember there was a saying which I would often repeat whenever I saved money. When evaluating whether I should or should not buy a particular thing, I would say, "A penny saved is a penny earned." One day, my elder son, who was then more than 18 years old, went with my younger son to purchase something from the market and chose to park the car in the common parking area, where the charges were 10 rupees, instead of the special parking area where the charges were 25 rupees. He justified this act by repeating the same maxim that "a penny saved is a penny earned," which my younger son shared, laughingly, with me.

10. If you want your children to respect the other elders in the family, you, as parents, must make sure that you talk in a positive manner about each other's parents and relatives in front of your children. Because

children, by virtue of not having reached developmental milestones, can get confused. They may develop a negative feeling for their grandparents and other relatives because they are not aware of the fact that it is OK to love each other, to respect each other, and still have a difference of opinion. This understanding is something that needs to be developed in them by building their emotional intelligence.

> *Come what may, one should never ever, as a parent, try to manipulate the pure feelings of the children.*

Come what may, one should never ever, as a parent, try to manipulate the pure feelings of the children. Otherwise they become very confused regarding what is wrong and what is right. Later on in their lives, they may develop a feeling of guilt as well and may blame the parents for manipulating their emotions.

11. Children actually feel very secure when there are set routines to follow. So, as parents, we must make sure that, as far as possible, we have routines in place, so that our children get into the habit of following routines simply by watching us. It is acceptable to have one or two odd days where there are no routines to follow, when everybody can relax and unwind.

12. As adults, you can have a great impact when you express how you feel yourself and communicate freely with one another. The most important thing is to hear out the other's point of view without being judgmental, critical, or a solution provider. The children will soon develop the habit of becoming empathetic listeners. You never know, one day your child might even become a counsellor!

13. People need people, and it is not unusual to see two people work harmoniously, in spite of having a difference of opinion. This needs to be followed by you as parents. Even though, as an individual, you may differ in your opinion, but on certain aspects of parenting you must agree with each other. Your children will, then, automatically learn to accept individual differences and turn out to be more accommodative of different points of view of other individuals. This will help in developing their emotional intelligence.

14. When your children see you stable in turbulent times, that is, being able to gather yourself after a failure and try once again; take each failure, setback, or loss in your stride; go down and again come back with great emotional strength, exhibiting strong resilience, they definitely feel empowered and believe that even they can be resilient when they go through testing times. I recollect my own experience—when we lost

our loved ones, how my mother had gathered her emotional strength and invested her time in us, that is, my brother and I. Now I was in her shoes and I was inspired by how she had taken care of us, her children. In a similar manner, I gathered myself and came back to life even after the tragic losses of my loved ones. As parents, every action of yours has an impact on your children, because you are their world, though you may be just another human being to others.

15. Accept changes readily. Even when I am writing this, I know this is easier said than done. But it is the truth that in life change is the only thing that is permanent, though we all dread change—including me. As parents, whether you react aggressively or respond intuitively to change, your actions will have an impact on your children. Therefore, we must make an effort to accept the perpetual changes in our life, readily. Our children will follow our example.

Given below are some of my experiences as a counsellor:

Case 1

Once a parent came to me and said that her child, Rahul, aged 3 years, did not eat fruits and wanted to know what she could do. She said that she had tried everything, but nothing seemed to have worked.

On questioning, I came to know that the parents were doing everything to feed the child fruits, except by being role models. Both the husband and wife disliked fruits, but they were very particular that their child had fruits. I gave them the advice that they needed to lead rather than push the child. This meant that the parents must become good role models by eating fruits themselves. Over a period of time, the entire family started enjoying fruits together and Rahul had now started wanting to eat the very fruit which his dad was eating.

Case 2

A parent said that her son, Aryan, who was 3 years and 8 months old, refused to listen to his mother or any other significant adult, whether at home or in his preschool. The mother wanted to know how to handle this.

On detailed interaction, I came to know that the mother, in spite of being a stay-at-home Mom, was always multitasking and therefore did not give focussed attention to the child. She was also very critical in her approach when listening. She would hardly let the child speak and express himself and did not respond appropriately. So the child thought that this was the correct way to interact when people spoke. He started imitating his mother's style.

It was only after the mother started to listen to the child without being judgmental, with the correct kind of eye contact, that the child also started responding by listening to what his mother had to say. This could happen only after the mother started practising being a proper listener.

Case 3

This is a case of Mehul, who was 4 years old. The parent said that child hated school.

Upon a detailed discussion, I found that the parents had a lot of complaints themselves against the school and the teachers, which they would discuss openly in front of the child. Over a period of time, the child absorbed the negative feelings of parents. Their mistrust of the school manifested itself as hatred in the child for the school.

After my advice, the parents discussed their concerns with the school authorities and sorted out their problems. Thus, the communication gap was resolved. I also advised them to speak positive things about the school in front of the child. Once this happened, the child became happy and settled down in the school. When the parents showed trust and belief in the school, it had a very positive impact on the child. He felt motivated to go to school and would really look forward to being there.

> *The parents were doing everything to feed the child fruits, except by being role models. Both the husband and wife disliked fruits, but they were very particular that their child had fruits.*

Case 4

There was a parent who said that her daughter, Rakshita, aged 2 years and 6 months, was scared of strangers. She did not let even her own relatives come near her.

After a detailed session, I came to know that the mother had been practicing fear based parenting, unintentionally. This had made the child very insecure and she became scared of every stranger. The mother had to consciously work to undo the impact of her actions by not scaring the child into doing things. It took a very long time for the child to be able to feel comfortable with strangers.

4

Mealtime Challenges

In my entire experience of counselling and conducting workshops, I have found that one of the most common concerns of parents is always related to food and their children. Mealtimes make the parents very anxious due to power struggles between the parent and the child at those times.

The fact is that the parents need to ensure that the mealtime should never become a battleground. Parents, without realizing, indulge in bribing, coaxing, or inducing fear psychosis, so that by hook or by crook, their child eats something at least. Parent-child relationship becomes at risk due to parents being over-enthusiastic and, unknowingly, pushing their child to eat.

This concern has definitely been impacted by the changing family system. Nuclear families, where both the parents are working, often have only one or two children. With so many challenges, where both the parents are constantly multitasking and are hard pressed for time, the mealtime of their child has become a big-time task to handle.

Most of the parents complain that their child does not eat at all or, if he or she does, then the process takes an hour or so. Where the child is fed separately, prior to the dinner time of the rest of the family, it becomes a huge task. The mother either moves along with the child from room to room, trying to feed him or her, or feeds the child by switching on the television, so that the child eats while watching a programme. Children become so engrossed in viewing the television that they are completely clueless about what they are eating.

Mealtimes, though very challenging for the parents of a pre-schooler, are very important for the overall development of the child. Children need a balanced meal for their proper growth and development and to remain healthy, so that they develop a good immunity to fight infections. Only a balanced meal will give them energy and make them feel good.

As parents, the mealtime of your child should be regarded as a sacred activity. The entire experience needs to be made enjoyable. Children love to explore and learn from every experience. This is applicable here as well. Children want to touch, play, roll the food; they want to smell, taste, and make sounds with their food. Therefore, within reasonable limits, we must allow them to explore the food and to interact with it first, before expecting them to eat it. In fact, messing up with food is an integral part of developing permanent eating patterns and children should be allowed to do so.

The need for you, the parents, is to have more and more patience. Eating habits and attitudes learned during childhood can last a lifetime. A child's mealtime behaviour can get drastically affected by unusual excitement, for example, during travelling, when visitors are there at home, in hot and humid weather, teething, during illness, or even when the child is emotionally upset. All these may increase or decrease his or her appetite.

> *As parents, the mealtime of your child should be regarded as a sacred activity. The entire experience needs to be made enjoyable.*

The food intake of the children is directly related to their activity levels as well. Children who lead a sedentary lifestyle will not be as hungry as children who go for outdoor activities. Researches in this field show that the growth of a pre-schooler is at a slower rate than an infant. This is why the appetite of your child may decrease in preschool years, so please do not worry.

Let us look at some strategies which have been very useful to parents in reducing the mealtime challenges of their children:

1. Never ever force-feed the child anything, especially milk, at a time when the child is stressed and has other anxieties to deal with, like in the morning time, before going to school. Milk has a complex protein, which

takes a longer time to digest when the child is under stress. In that case, children are less likely to finish their tiffin, because they would be feeling full. Milk, if taken at a more relaxed time, gets easily digested.

2. Refrain from bottle-feeding milk to your child. It is surprising that, in spite of the fact that paediatricians do not recommend bottle-feeding, still parents, for their own convenience, do so. In cases where there is extensive bottle-feeding, ranging from three times in a day, and often even if only once or twice, children refuse to eat. Because of the liquid taken, the stomach feels full and the child hardly takes any solid food. Children who are fed sweetened milk at night, before going to sleep, are prone to developing dental caries, because while they are sleeping with the bottle in their mouth, the liquid pools around the teeth, subjecting the teeth to many kinds of bacterial infections. So make sure you do away with this habit, as soon as possible.

3. Arrange family meals where you let your child eat with you. Let the child use the same kind of plate as yours, instead of a baby plate. It will be more enjoyable for your child and you will get an opportunity to talk about food, its variety, colour, and so on.

4. Do not ever puree food in a mixer and then feed it to the child. In one instance, when a child was served food in a normal manner,

Mealtime Challenges

he refused to eat it, saying that he never ate that food, because he always got to see only semi-solid food in a puree form.

5. Whenever you are serving food or packing tiffin for your child, make sure that you give child-sized portions only. Children feel very frustrated when they cannot finish their food, like their friends. They start feeling that there is something wrong with them, since they cannot finish their food or tiffin. This impacts their self-esteem negatively.

6. Involve your child in the process of serving food. This really works wonders. When serving food at lunch or dinner time, get the child to help you lay the table, talk excitedly about food, and allow the child to serve his or her own food in the plate. You will be surprised to see that your child has completely finished the food in the plate. This is because the child was involved and felt in control.

7. As far as the tiffin is concerned, involve the child by sitting together and preparing a tiffin menu for the week. Give the child options to choose from. This could look something like this:

Proposed menu for the week
   i) Monday: *Parantha* and a seasonal vegetable
   ii) Tuesday: Rice day

iii) Wednesday: My favourite

iv) Thursday: Sandwich day

v) Friday: Pancake day (Anything like a *chila* made out of *besan*, *sooji*, rice, or dals, with a blend of vegetables)

Seasonal fruits: one or two pieces can be given daily. There can be many versions of this menu, keeping in mind your family's eating habits.

This really works. I tried this with my children and it worked very well—to the extent that I could not change what was there in the menu plan without keeping the children informed. If I did not inform, the tiffin would come back!

8. Do not put too many restrictions in the name of table manners when your child is making an effort to become independent at the task of eating. Children who are corrected too much on the dining table are less likely to be happy about mealtimes and may simply want to avoid the whole process. Remember, they will learn table manners, but if they are not allowed to experiment with the food, they may not be too interested in eating, which may remain a challenge for life.

9. Pre-schoolers need to eat small, frequent meals throughout the day because they have small stomachs and high energy needs.

10. Give snacks one or two hours before meals so that they don't interfere with the meals.

Mealtime Challenges

11. Have healthy snack options at home. Do not keep chips, candies, chocolates, etc., at home. If they need to be kept, make sure you keep them out of your child's view. Children tend to eat whatever is there in their view and if you say "no" to them, it gets both of you into the unpleasant world of power struggle.

> *Do not put too many restrictions in the name of table manners when your child is making an effort to become independent at the task of eating.*

12. Do not give too much preference to messy or difficult to eat food in the tiffin, like noodles and pasta. Besides having little nutrition, children find it very challenging to handle such messy food, because they are still developing their fine motor skills.

13. Do not make the TV the mealtime babysitter. Your child might eat the food that you are trying to feed while watching TV, but will hardly come to know about the food being eaten and, therefore, it is not a solution to the larger spectrum of mealtime challenges which will keep coming to you regularly.

14. Children generally love routine and feel secure in it. So it will be a great idea to follow mealtime routines and let the child look forward to them.

15. Make sure your child has fruits instead of fruit juices and plenty of water during the day to avoid going through the painful experience of constipation, which is very common at this age, if you are not conscious about it.

16. Above all, let your child feel hungry before mealtimes. Do not overstuff the child just before a meal, because it gives you satisfaction and takes care of the guilt that you might be having because of not spending enough time with him or her. Instead, let the child demand food and enjoy the whole experience.

Given below are some of my experiences as a counsellor:

Case 1

A mother came to me saying that her child Dushyant, who was 2 years and 3 months old, was not interested in eating and threw a lot of tantrums after coming back from his preschool. This was a regular behaviour since the child joined preschool.

After a detailed discussion, I found that both the parents were working. The mother had an afternoon shift. Therefore, when the child returned from school, the mother would be in a hurry, but felt that her job would only be complete if she fed the child, whereas the child was neither in a rush nor was hungry enough at that time. Due to this, the child started detesting the whole experience.

I advised the mother to let the child eat when he was actually hungry and that the father could take care of the mealtime process and the problem got resolved.

Case 2

Once a parent came to me and said that her child Taneesha, aged 2 years and 2 months, did not eat anything at all.

You will be amazed to know that after questioning her, I found out that the child ate a cheese slice and a bar of chocolate every day. Then how could she feel hungry? There was no space in her stomach for nutritious and healthy foods. It was only when the mother did away with the chocolate and cheese slice did the child actually start having proper meals.

Case 3

Once, a parent came and told me that her child Mayank, aged 3 and a half years, did not eat any food that she packed for him in the tiffin and came back hungry and irritated from preschool. But he ate readily when she fed him.

On asking for information, I found that the child had always been given pureed food, which was in a semi-solid state. He had never seen solid food and feared that it would get stuck in his throat.

After my advice, the mother stopped mashing and pureeing the child's food. She started giving solid, whole foods at home. She also started involving the child in the process. Thus the child could overcome his phobia. Even a fifteen month old child is capable enough to eat on his or her own.

Case 4

There was a case of Malini, who was 2 and a half years old. The parents' said that their child started crying at the very thought or the slightest mention of food.

After discussion, I found that both the mother and the father were great perfectionists. They carried this trait even to the dining table. The child was often rebuked for dropping food particles on the table, not using a knife and fork properly, and was forced to eat too much food because the parents felt the child did not know how much was enough for her overall growth.

After my advice the parents became more child friendly and relaxed at the dining table. They allowed the child to serve herself, eat on her own, and stopped being critical of her table manners. The child then stopped crying on the mention of food.

5

Validate Your Child's Emotions

I feel emotional validation is one of the most important tools in the hands of parents, through the use of which they can develop a beautiful, strong, and healthy relationship with their children, for life. It is not so important what all you do for your children; it is much more important how you make them feel at various points in their lives when they are going through a challenging situation. Children will remember us for how we made them feel. As parents, it is our duty to talk about how we feel and not shy away from our feelings. Even if we are feeling unhappy, we need to talk about our feelings.

As parents, we need to validate the feelings of our children. We need to tell them that it is OK to cry, it is OK to feel frustrated, it is OK to feel angry, it is OK to feel hurt. At the same time, we have to give them tools to resolve the problem. Also, when we share with our children how hurt we were in a particular situation and tell them that now we have come out of it and are feeling much better and also discuss our coping strategy with them, the children feel they can also achieve the same. Once they see their parents have negative feelings and see them coming out of them, they feel even they can do this, because parents are their entire world.

Setting up an emotional tone in the home is extremely important for children. This means that everyone at home talks about their feelings, without the others in the family commenting, criticizing, or being judgmental.

As parents of our two sons, we would get together on weekends, perform an activity in which we would ask our sons to highlight those emotions of ours, during the week, which they did not approve of and why. This exercise was an eye opener for us and we got a feedback about those emotions of ours which were inconsistent with our role as parents. Since it was a group activity, our sons also asked us to point out their emotions which we did not approve of. At times, we would joke and laugh at our own actions. Since nobody was critical or judgmental, and we were all relaxed, it was a reflective feedback to all of us. We would all try to correct our behaviour in the coming week.

The moment we, as parents, start acknowledging the feelings of our children, they start feeling very secure in the environment created. The children then feel free to express their positive and negative feelings alike, because the healthy emotional environment provided by the parents is without any preconditions or judgements.

As parents, we have unknowingly been conditioned to provide solutions to our children, get judgmental, or become critical about what they feel and say. Instead, most of the time what the children need is empathetic listening and a signal from us that it is OK to feel the way they are feeling at that point in time.

> *This definitely means that you must see the whole picture before passing a judgment as a parent.*

Let us look at some tried and tested strategies which will help you to validate your child's emotions and set up an emotional tone in the house:

1. Whenever your child cries and says, "No, I don't want to go to school," never ever say, what we often say to the child, that is, "Son, you must go to school. Look at your sister, she goes to school happily. Look at your friend, he goes to school readily and does not ever cry." You may have the best intentions to help the child but, unknowingly, what you convey at the emotional level to the child is, "I do not accept you or your feelings the way you are. I want you to be like your friend or like your sister, who do not cry and go to school willingly." This adds to the problem and the self-esteem of the child gets still more affected, with another challenge and competition from the sister and the friend, even though your intention was to simply motivate the child to go to school.

2. When your child does not want to recite rhymes, sing songs, or dance, etc., in front of visitors, refrain from the urge to say, "If you don't do it, how will these people know that you are a smart child, a good child, and an intelligent child?" What you can say is, "It is OK if you do not want to come now. In case you feel like it, you can come and meet your aunt and uncle and mummy will be eagerly waiting for you."

3. Whenever there is a complaint of your child, do not start a one-sided show by joining the other party. Whether the complaint is from the school or a neighbour, do not hurt the self-esteem of the child by rebuking him or her for the act straightaway. First, listen calmly. Try to hear both the sides of the story to understand what exactly happened. Be supportive if your child had no other option but to act the way he or she did at that point in time. This does not mean that you are being defensive, but this definitely means that you must see the whole picture before passing a judgment as a parent. You were not around when that incident happened and you need to consider all the facts first.

4. If your child does not perform well at a particular competition and is upset about it, you, in a bid to help the child, should never say, "Come on, be a sport and cheer up!" It would be more emotionally soothing for the child if you could say, "It is OK to feel upset in such a situation. Even I felt very upset

when I was in a similar situation. And just like me, you will also come out of it and feel better."

5. Treat your child as an individual having an independent mind of his or her own. Never take your child for granted, ask for permissions as you would from an adult. For example, if you are going to the market, ask if he or she wants to accompany you or not. Then prepare the child in advance about what all will happen in the market and also your expectations from the child.

6. Never ever force your child to share his or her toys with your friend's child, especially if they have dropped in all of a sudden to call on you. Do not emotionally blackmail the child by saying, "If you are not going to share your toys, Mummy will not talk to you." Instead, you could say, "I understand you do not want to share this toy, but, with your permission, can I give another toy to this friend of yours? I will really be thankful to you." If you do this, your child will give you a pleasant surprise.

7. There will be times when your child enrols for an activity, which he or she had earlier desired, but does not want to continue. Though you have spent money for it, please do not force your child to continue. You should find out the cause of the change of mind. If the reason is genuine, stop sending the child for that activity. The neuron

connections which had to happen because of that activity might have been completed. When that happens, children start looking for new experiences to be able to initiate new connections of neurons.

8. Whatever your children say, have faith and belief in them. Listen to what they say, however weird it may be. Do not shut them out. If you make fun of their concerns or criticize them, they will not come back to you and the door to their emotional life be shut for you, for ever.

9. As parents, it is extremely important that we do not compare our own children with one another. We should not compare our children with other children either. Accept your children, wholeheartedly, for what they are.

10. It is not a great idea to expose your children to fairy tales or mythological stories before they are six years old. This is because they are in the developmental phase and are not equipped to distinguish fantasy from reality before that age. We can all check the correctness of this by the following example: When I say "stepmother" what image comes to your mind? I am sure the immediate feelings are negative. A stepmother is often imagined as someone wicked. And where did this image come from? Obviously, from the fairy tales which we read as children—

even though we know that they are a fantasy. I remember feeling very scared and sad whenever I would hear or read the story of Shravan Kumar and his blind parents, or a Prahlad story, or Ramayan, or Mahabharat, because of the fighting and violence involved.

> *Whatever your children say, have faith and belief in them. Listen to what they say, however weird it may be.*

11. As a parent, you must never get into an ego conflict with your children. They may say hurtful things to you, but remember they actually do not mean them, so do not go by the literal meaning. Understand the hidden emotion. Often, because they are feeling upset and don't know what to do, they indulge in such acts.

I have to confess that, as a mother, I am my sons' emotional pillow, where they can vent out all sorts of negative emotions, as well as positive ones. I rejoice in this status, because this is the only way to be able to understand what my children are going through. If you become alarmed, they might zip up their emotions and you may never come to know what they feel in a particular situation.

Given below are some of my experiences as a counsellor:

Case 1

There was a case of a child, Vivek, 3 years and 10 months old. The mother was getting constant complaints from the teacher that the child was hitting and pushing other children. The mother, without going in to the details of the case, on the provocation from the teacher, told the child, "I am very embarrassed due to your behaviour. If you continue like this, I will not talk to you or love you." Over a period of time, the child became reluctant to go to school and started behaving aggressively with the other children of his class as well.

I advised the mother to start validating the emotions of the child. Then she came to know that her child was being bullied by other children in the class, due to which he, in his self-defence, would indulge in acts like hitting and pushing. When he approached the teacher, she would say "I don't want to hear any complaints."

Once the mother started validating the child's feelings, he started getting better and, together as a team, the teacher and the mother could help the child get rid of his aggressive behaviour.

Case 2

A parent's close friend complained that her son, Samarth, 4 years and 1 month old, had slapped and pushed her daughter. Without even making an effort to know what actually transpired between the two children, Samarth's mother started scolding her son,

Validate Your Child's Emotions

saying how he had ruined her friendship. The child wanted to say something, but the mother was in no mood to listen to him.

It was only when she met another friend, who was a witness to the incident, that she came to know that her friend's daughter had first snatched her son's ball and pushed Samarth. In retaliation, he had slapped the girl and pushed her as well, after which she had started crying. When her protective mother came to her rescue, the girl put the blame on Samarth.

Samarth's mother went home and said sorry to her son. She made an effort to validate what all he was going through at an emotional level. She promised him that, in future, she would always listen to him first, to understand why he behaved in a particular manner. Samarth felt comforted, safe, and secure in his knowledge that, come what may, his mother was approachable and he could talk to her for anything and everything.

Case 3

Agam, at the age of 3 years and 10 months, remained quiet and did not share or talk much to the adults at home, that is, his Mom and Dad. He would hardly interact with his peer group at school. The teacher was worried and discussed this with the parents. They were all concerned, but did not know how to help the child.

After a long session with them, I came to know that the parents were perfectionists. They were always correcting, criticizing, and judging the child, due to which the child had become withdrawn and would not make any effort to interact with his parents at home, to avoid their negative comments. At school he remained timid and quiet because, in a bid to control his behaviour and ensure he was disciplined in the class, the parents would often indulge in fear based parenting. They would tell the child that if he talked to friends or made noise, the teacher would punish him and she would not keep him in her class.

Once the parents understood where they were going wrong, they made the required efforts to change. Soon, the same child became very lively and playful. To achieve this, the parents had to undo what they had initially put in his subconscious mind. It took about one and a half months to see the change in his behaviour. Both the parents and the teacher had to work hand in hand to rebuild the self-esteem of the child.

Case 4

This is the case of Kavya, aged 2 years 9 months, who, after joining preschool, backtracked on her toilet training. The mother became very anxious about this. She would often belittle the child by saying, "See what you have done in spite of being such a big girl. Shame, shame! How could you wet your pants? Are you a small baby?" She would also tell her in-laws, who would make fun of her. This made the situation worse. Instead of the problem getting better, it started deteriorating. The self-esteem of the child became very low and the child started refusing to go to the school.

After the counselling, the parents changed their approach. The mother would tell the daughter, "It is OK. Accidents do happen. Come, let me help you change

Validate Your Child's Emotions

and I am sure you'll come out of this habit." And the father gave his example that, when he was a baby, he would also often have such accidents at school and at home as well. But, slowly and gradually, he came out of it. The child then felt reassured that she need not be scared of her parents or embarrassed about her act. It had happened to her dad as well. If he could come out of it, so would she.

> *The child then felt reassured that she need not be scared of her parents or embarrassed about her act.*

6

Your Child's Sleep Time

According to the National Sleep Foundation, USA, children in the age group of 3–5 need about 11 to 13 hours of sleep every night. Many preschool children also nap during the day for about one to two hours every day. It is better if the children sleep continuously for 10–11 hours every night, rather than sleeping in bits and pieces during the day.

Once the children start school, many parents, out of concern, forcibly make them sleep in the afternoon, thinking that they are helping them, since they are such tiny creatures and must have got tired after attending school.

There are some parents whose children are highly energetic. They make them sleep in the afternoon to get some peace, because they are not equipped enough to creatively channelize the energies of these children. This has an opposite effect. The children feel more energized when they wake up. They are wide awake till midnight and refuse to sleep at all.

In my opinion children, if they fall asleep on their own in the afternoon, should be allowed to take a one-hour nap. The ones who are not interested in sleeping should be engaged in some meaningful activity to facilitate more connections of their neurons. Do not force your children to take a nap in the afternoon just because others are doing it. Every child is unique and has a different body clock.

Pre-schoolers like routines and prefer consistency in their schedules. So it is a good idea to have routines which the child looks forward to. But then, these routines need to be followed. As parents, we need to figure out what works best for our child and, accordingly, plan a schedule for the day. Involve the child in the planning so that he or she really looks forward to it. To keep the child busy when he or she does not want to sleep, have a planned activity ready, keeping the mental age of the child in mind. Be enthusiastic about it, so that the child really looks forward to this activity. Research says that children often tend to sleep when they get bored and there is not enough stimulation in the environment. So take care of this when planning or conducting the activities.

Let us look at some strategies to maximize on healthy sleep patterns:

1. Do not have television or other onscreen devices in the bedroom of the child.
2. To induce sleep, do not allow bottle-feeding. When children sleep while feeding on milk, they may get ear infection as well problems

with teeth. Never force your child to sleep if he or she does not want to sleep.

3. If your child has gone off to sleep in the afternoon, do not wait for him or her to get up on their own. Wake them up after one hour, or at the most, after two hours.

4. For those children who do not prefer to sleep in the afternoon, have some "quiet time" where the environment is relaxed, with minimum stimulations. This could be reading a book, or looking at a picture book, or telling a story, which will be refreshing for the child.

5. Children should not watch television at least one hour prior to sleep. This will give them time to calm down the stimulations of the mind to enable a smooth sleep.

6. Children must be taken for outdoor activities every day for at least two hours in the evening. They are growing physically and need to exercise their gross motor skills, that is, the bigger muscles of the body.

7. To facilitate and ensure proper sleep routines, make sure the room is dark, but do switch on a night lamp if the child is not comfortable in the dark. Many pre-schoolers have fear of the dark. Have some activities which help the brain to relax, like narrating a story or listening to some soft music. Make sure the sleep-time stories revolve around the world of children, that is, stories related

to animals, sharing, friends, family, and so on. Make sure there is no violence in the story and no negative actions like death and killing or separation from the parents, because this goes into their subconscious mind and may negatively impact the sleep by making the child anxious. Don't expect your child to switch off immediately and go to sleep. Allow him or her enough transition time.

> *Children should not watch television at least one hour prior to sleep. This will give them time to calm down the stimulations of the mind to enable a smooth sleep.*

8. Never ever coax the child to sleep by inducing fear, saying, "If you do not sleep, the Guard will come and take you," or, "*Buddha Baba* will come and take you."

9. Make sure your child does not take any food with caffeine before sleeping time because caffeine can become over-stimulating for the child and create hindrance in the sleep routine.

10. Let your child snuggle in with his or her attachment toy or a blanket or a stuffed toy in the bed.

11. It is a fact that children thrive on routines and feel very secure with them. Try to follow the same bedtime and the same wake-up time, as far as possible, every day.

Given below are some of my experiences as a counsellor:

Case 1

Parents of Sagiri, aged 3 years and 9 months, said that their child did not sleep till well past midnight and then found it difficult to wake up for school the next morning. They wondered what they could do.

After a detailed discussion, I found that the child, while watching TV, went to sleep in the afternoon every day, for about three to four hours. In the evening, she played a little in the house and then watched TV till late night, as they had television in their bedroom.

After counselling, the parents made drastic changes in the child's schedule. First of all, they took out the television from the bedroom. Then, slowly and gradually, they reduced the duration of the afternoon sleep. Later, they were asked to completely do away with Sagiri's afternoon nap, because the child was not sleeping on her own but had to be made to sleep forcibly. The parents were also advised to take Sagiri for outdoor activities and bring consistency and set sleep routines for the child. In about three months' time, most of the concerns of the parents had been taken care of.

Case 2

In the case of a Shreya, aged 2 years and 10 months, she would go to sleep at 6 p.m. in the evening and got up at 9 p.m. Then she would refuse to sleep till midnight. It had become a major concern for the parents.

On questioning, I found that the child was hardly engaged in any physical activity. She watched TV in the evening, after which the mother bottle-fed her with milk. While she was bottle-feeding, she would often go off to sleep.

On advice, the parents made a very conscious effort to change. They removed the bottle-feed completely. The mother started taking her daughter to the park, where she enjoyed playing with her friends. The mother made sure her daughter was taken to the park at 5.30 p.m. and by the time it was 6 p.m., her usual sleep time, she would be so excited and busy with her friends that she completely forgot about her sleep. In about two months, her sleep time got shifted to about 8.30 p.m. in the evening and then she could sleep properly till about 6 a.m. in the morning.

Case 3

There was a case of a couple where the father was a businessman. He came home at 10 p.m. The mother made sure that their daughter, Nisha, aged 3 years and 11 months, slept well during the day so that she could be awake when the father returned home. The entire family never slept before 1 a.m. As a result, the child got up late in the morning and was always late for school. Often, she would be absent from the class. Due to the irregular attendance of the child, she could not understand the concepts being taught in the class. She felt disoriented and started lagging behind in the class work, which her friends were able to do effortlessly. The parents were really worried and anxious.

It was only after several counselling sessions that they accepted the facts and made the necessary changes in the schedule of the child. The situation got better only after four months. The mother made changes so that the child slept by 8.30 p.m. Then she started getting up fresh in the morning and was happy to go to school.

Case 4

Viraj, aged 2 years and 10 months, would refuse to sleep. He would fight with sleep even when feeling extremely sleepy. Also, he refused to sleep in bed, preferring to sleep on the sofa. The mother had tried everything, but nothing seemed to work. She was very anxious when she came to me for counselling.

On trying to understand the case, I came to know that the child had backtracked on toilet training since he had started school. The mother, instead of helping the child, ridiculed and scared him so that he did not wet his bed. The entire bedtime or sleep routine became a very scary thing for the child. Because of the over-anxiousness of the mother, the child did not want to sleep in his bed.

Your Child's Sleep Time

After counselling, the mother stopped ridiculing the child. I asked her to help the child by setting an alarm and by taking the child to the washroom during the night. The mother also started reassuring the child. She told him that, even she, as a child, had backtracked on toilet training initially when she joined preschool. But this became better and she could easily overcome it. This gave lot of comfort to the child and he started wanting to sleep in his bed and even stopped bed-wetting because the mother became relaxed about the whole matter.

What Is the Work of Your Child—Play, Learn, Eat, or Sleep?

The way we, the adults, have various businesses to look after, pre-schoolers are also busy throughout the day in their work, that is, play, learn, eat, and sleep. During my interactions with parents, I have asked this question innumerable times—according to them, what is their priority out of the four activities of the child? Most of the parents said eating was their first priority, learning as second, sleeping as the third, and playing the last. You may be surprised to know that, according to research studies, playing is the first priority of the child.

Playing is a serious business for children. As they play, they learn. After playing and learning, they are hungry, so eating comes third in their list and their last priority is sleeping.

Children love playing. Some of us think that it is a waste of time, but actually, every act of play of a child has a purpose behind it. While they are playing, they are learning problem solving skills, they are honing creativity, they are developing imagination, they are developing fine and gross motor skills, they are developing social and emotional skills, they are learning language and cognitive skills, and, above all, the neurons in their brain are getting connected with each experience of theirs for establishing learning pathways.

To sum up, I would say that playing helps in channelizing energies of children and helps in their overall and holistic development.

Children like active play where the enjoyment comes from getting involved directly. In the absence of active play, they enjoy passive play, where the enjoyment comes by observing the activities of others. Their favourite passive play is onscreen activities. The home environment, where they spend 80 per cent of the time, should allow maximum opportunities for play, which should be both active and passive, to facilitate their overall growth.

During the process of play, you will see that children are engrossed completely in what they are doing. Almost always, they initiate the activity on their own, experience great happiness and joy, are curious, and engaged in exploring. Almost all the activities which are self-initiated by children are examples of play.

Let us look at some of the strategies to support and facilitate the important task of promoting and supporting play of our children:

1. Make sure your children go out every day for outdoor play, at least for 1–2 hours, where they get to interact with their peer group. Peer group interaction is a very important part of play in this age group. Make sure that during this outdoor play, they hop, run, jump, and exercise their gross motor skills. They should not only be restricted to the swings area, because that will hardly meet the criteria of outdoor activity.

2. Give your children ample opportunities for unstructured play. For example, when you are replacing bedcovers, let your children use the discarded ones to construct an imaginary house under the table. The cushion and pillow covers can be used to create a path, and so on. Unstructured play is a stimulant to creativity and self insight. Children love it. If you reflect on your childhood days, you will realize that you, too, have benefited from it.

3. If your child has constructed some imaginary play out of something very strange, do not only look at the end product. Ask the child what he or she has made and validate the process. Initiating a conversation around play is very important. Never ever make fun of the work of the child or ridicule him or her for being messy—this action of yours might suppress the creativity of the child.

What Is the Work of Your Child—Play, Learn, Eat, or Sleep?

4. Resist the peer pressure of enrolling your children in structured play like a karate, cricket, or a swimming class, unless your child is very keen on it. It is not about anybody else, but about you and your child. Do whatever your child is comfortable with. And go ahead only after you have involved the child in the decision-making.

   > *Give your children ample opportunities for unstructured play.*

5. Have a separate play area for your child to which he or she can look forward to and have a quiet time there.

6. Children are very fond of playing with music, water, and sand. They love exploring and playing with colours. So make sure you give them exposure to all this.

7. Let your children play with utensils and let them design their own unique ways of playing. They cannot go on playing with the same toy again and again because the neuron connections that had to happen because of that exposure have happened. They cannot go on repeating that connection. Instead, they look forward to something different, which could even be playing with the same toy in a different manner.

8. On a daily basis, mothers should set aside some time, which you can call "Mummy and Baby time". During this time, play with your child, but ask the child to lead rather than you. You will be amazed at the multifaceted benefits of this time of togetherness.

9. Let your children scribble and draw. It is a great idea to have chart papers pasted on the walls all around the house, up to the child's height, so that they can have a space of their own for expressing themselves and feel proud to share their work with friends and relatives.

10. Children love to play with dry and wet flour. You can spread a newspaper on the floor and tape the sides. Then you and your child can make as much mess as you feel like. It will be a lifetime experience.

11. Children learn a lot through imitative play and role play, where they like to dress up and admire themselves. Children love to watch themselves. Having a child sized mirror in the house is a good idea. The mirror should be of the child's height, at the eye level of the child.

12. Since children love messing up, you can sometimes have "newspaper rains". Collect a lot of newspapers. Both of you can tear these into small pieces and throw them in the air. And then both of you can pick up

the pieces and throw them again. Children simply love this game.

13. Set up water play for your children. In summers, before they take a bath, fill a tumbler with water. Put some plastic glasses of different colours and let them play with them. They love pouring water from one tumbler to another. This play facilitates fine motor development.

14. Children love playing "tea party". They love imitating whatever their mothers do in the kitchen. This must be encouraged, because children move from known to unknown, even when it comes to play.

15. Children are really excited about verbal play, where you can ask them to scream, sing, or make silly sounds.

16. Play hide and seek with them by hiding their toys, dolls, and puzzles. They will simply love it.

17. Use shaving cream or toothpaste to create figures on a window pane or mirror. Children really enjoy this.

18. Involve your children in the household chores and do some cooking together.

19. Have easel boards, paints, and brushes in place and you'll be amazed to see the artist in your child.

Given below are some of my experiences as a counsellor:

Case 1

Nalini, aged 4 years, would always be cranky and never want to go for the dance class which her mother had put her into. The mother kept wondering what was wrong.

On discussion, I found that the child had a set of friends with whom she was very friendly. She wanted to play in the evening with them. Since she had joined her dance classes, she could not do so. So the dance class had become a pressure on Nalini.

Once we figured this out, the mother stopped sending her to the dance class. She allowed her child to go for unstructured play with her friends in the park, where they would gather leaves, run behind butterflies, and observe the ants. Over a period of time, Nalini became the original happy and cheerful child that she was.

Case 2

Once a parent came to me and said that her daughter, Divya, was becoming more aggressive with each passing day. She was hitting everybody, including her parents. This had started since the child had begun going to school.

The discussions revealed that there was no outdoor play in the daily routine of the child. When I asked the reason from the mother, she said that she felt that the child had a long day at school, so must be getting tired.

So she did not send her to play, unlike earlier, before she had joined preschool.

It was only when I explained that the mother understood that her child required a lot of movement, which was hardly there in her daily routine. So the child's energies were not being channelized. To vent out her energy, she would often hit and push. She became aggressive because she felt restless. She could not verbalize her problem and neither could the mother realize it.

After the session, the mother understood the needs of her daughter better. She made sure that the child was given enough opportunity for physical activity and to learn. When this started happening, the child stopped being aggressive.

> She allowed her child to go for unstructured play with her friends in the park, where they would gather leaves, run behind butterflies, and observe the ants.

Case 3

This is a case of a mother who was very ambitious about the development of her son, Sameer, aged 3 years and 11 months. She had micromanaged every minute of her child's life. After preschool, the child was going to a music class, swimming class, and an art class. The child would hardly get any time for unstructured play and peer group interaction. Due to this, he started throwing tantrums. He became very stubborn, which was very challenging for the mother.

After the advice, the mother stopped pushing the child from one activity to the other. She started spending some meaningful "me time" with the child and allowing some unstructured play. All this had a positive effect and the situation improved significantly.

Case 4

Once a parent came with a concern that her daughter, Kirti, aged 3 years and 2 months, did not eat enough, did not want to sleep, and always wanted the company of an adult. She would start screaming whenever other children tried coming near her.

After a long discussion, I found that the child had an apparently perfect routine. At home, they had a full time maid and grandparents to look after Kirti. She was the only child with eight adults at home, including all the support staff. Obviously, everybody would pamper the baby of the house. But this was also the cause of the problem! Due to all this attention from adults, Kirti felt very threatened in the company of her little friends. Moreover, when she went to the park in the evening, for an hour or so, she would hardly get off the swings.

After counselling, the mother started accompanying the child to the park, where she made a conscious effort to make friends with other parents and making sure that her child started interacting and playing with the other children of her age group. Since the child started playing and running, she could exhaust her surplus energy and so looked forward to her meals, slept well, and started enjoying the company of her friends.

8

Is Your TV a Babysitter?

Once a preschool child was asked by the teacher as to what he would like to become when he grew up. Pat came the reply, "Ma'am, I want to become the TV of my house!" On further probing by the teacher, the child said, "Ma'am, if I become the TV of my house, I will get to spend more time with my Mom and Dad, because they spend endless hours with the TV and then they don't have any time for me."

This situation is actually an occasion for reflection for all of us. We are the role models for our little ones. When we exhibit this attitude towards TV, then how can we stop our children from getting addicted to it?

TV viewing, along with other onscreen activities, is an integral part of a child's everyday life, as early as he or she is in the womb. Television can have a major impact on your child's development in a number of ways, primarily by taking time away from other activities needed for the physical, social, emotional, cognitive, and language development. This is the threat to today's society where we, maybe not by choice but due to lack of choice, have to use TV as a babysitter for our children.

Parents, in spite of all the junk food available, do we let our children eat it whenever they feel like or whenever they are hungry? I am sure none of us can even think of letting our children have junk food all the time. We make sure that our children, somehow or the other, have nutritious and balanced meals. This is because we know that food helps children to grow physically and we can see and measure this growth.

Unfortunately, we don't give the same attention to the mental growth of our children. Whatever children observe and hear is food for their mental growth. Giving the remote control of TV to children is like giving them junk mental food. The ill effects of this junk mental food start showing when the child starts using abusive language, becomes aggressive, imitates bad behaviour from bad role models on TV, and doesn't make friends. Today's child views an average of 200,000 acts of violence before he or she is 18 years old, reports the magazine *Kids Health*.

Unlimited and unmonitored TV viewing can reduce the attention span in children, distort their body image, create fear, increase aggression, and increase violence. Watching TV before bedtime can lead to sleep problems for pre-schoolers, according to a study in *Journal of Paediatrics*. Parents must turn the TV off at least 60 minutes before the children get tucked in to go to sleep.

Is Your TV a Babysitter?

TV viewing causes a hindrance in building imagination, exploration, and natural creativity of children. Children subjected to excessive TV viewing are less cooperative, less imaginative, and less enthusiastic about learning at school. Children who watch a lot of TV during early, formative years are at an increased risk of childhood obesity, poor social development, and aggressive behaviour.

> *TV viewing should not be more than one hour per day during the week and not more than three hours each on Saturday and Sunday.*

Let us look at some tried and tested methods to unplug our children from the menace of onscreen world:

1. Are you aware of how many hours you and your child are watching TV, in a week? If not, maintain a TV logbook for the family. Anybody who turns the TV on must log in the number of hours and minutes and what programme they have viewed. This will help you to understand the situation correctly.

2. After analysing the total TV viewing hours, make a goal. If your child is between 2–5 years old, TV viewing should not be more than one hour per day during the week and not more than three hours each on Saturday and Sunday. If your child is more than eight

years old, then it should not be more than two hours per day during the week and eight hours on weekends. Make your schedule accordingly and also post it in the TV room, along with the logbook.

3. Let there be only one TV in the house and not one TV in every room, which is the trend in almost every household. If you have the TV in the bedroom where your child sleeps, remove it at once and keep it elsewhere.

4. On weekends, sit with the child and select shows to be watched during the next week. Make a weekly schedule along with your child, which has been approved by you.

5. Turn the TV off after the programme is over. To adhere to this, use an alarm if required. This has been working well for me, because even as adults, we get carried away, start flipping channels, and forget to stick to time schedules.

6. Watch TV with your children to be able to have a conversation with them about what they saw and how they feel about it. It is very important for us, as parents, to be able to guide the emotions of our children. To be able to help our children, we need to understand and talk about how they feel.

7. Instead of lecturing, what will work is enrolling your child for an active hobby class that he or she has been interested in, like dance, a particular sport, or swimming, and so on.

8. TV viewing is passive play for children, because they derive the same enjoyment by watching TV as they would have achieved if they had been involved in active play. As a substitute, go for fun walks like word walk, nature walk, and other outdoor activities on a daily basis. Children need active play every day for about an hour or two.

9. You can arrange for "play dates" for your child with his or her friend by collaborating with another parent.

10. Be available and involved and see how your children will not ask even once for TV or laptop or your mobile. Take out your old photo albums and go down memory lane while browsing. You will wonder how time flies.

11. Spend time together, make a list of things your children want to do and post it on the refrigerator or near the TV.

12. Have some hands-on fun by bringing out clay or play dough and let your imagination run.

13. Have a "tickle party"—roll over and around the house with your kids.

14. Put a lot of good dress-up stuff near a mirror and let your children enjoy the make believe corner.

15. Play treasure hunt or "find the object". Hide a small toy somewhere and use the old hot-cold method to guide the seeker to the toy.

16. Let your child take a "play bath". Fill a tub with some water and toys. Let your child get in and just play.
17. Create a story together using a scrap book. Involve the child in colouring, pasting, cutting, and tearing.
18. Play photographer. Take some photos, do a wild and crazy photo shoot with your kids, dress up with some fun ideas and snap away.
19. Plant seeds together, see the progress of the plants, and take care of them.

Given below are some of my experiences as a counsellor:

Case 1

A mother came and said that her daughter, Bhavya, aged 4 years, did not want to go to school. But till a month ago, she was very happy and comfortable going to school.

During the discussion, the facts which came out were an eye-opener for the mother as well as for me. At the time when there were terrorist attacks at Mumbai, they were broadcast on TV continuously for two days. A minute by minute report of the entire episode was telecasted and both the Mom and Dad watched TV continuously at that time. This child was also around. The parents thought that since she was a baby and busy with her toys and in her own world, she would hardly understand what was going on.

Is Your TV a Babysitter?

Surprisingly, they were wrong. The child refused to go to school the next day. When they tried to push her, she started crying and saying, "Mummy, please let me stay at home. Otherwise terrorists will come and attack us." The exposure of the child to violence by terrorists happened by accident and not by design, but since the child's subconscious learning is best developed in this age, the child absorbed everything. She felt very insecure and therefore wanted to cling to the mother.

It was only when the mother understood how the accidental viewing had impacted the child's impressionable mind, could she become relaxed and not push the child. I advised her to validate the insecurity and fear which the child had. It was not before four weeks that we could see the difference.

The child was allowed to watch TV programmes which were positive. She was given the comfort that significant adults, that is, the parents and the teachers, could validate how she was feeling. The parents gave the child enough transition time to develop faith and belief in the environment and feel safe and secure. After all this, she actually started going to school.

> *The parents thought that since she was a baby and busy with her toys and in her own world, she would hardly understand what was going on. Surprisingly, they were wrong.*

Case 2

In this case, the parents were worried about their son, Shivansh, aged 2 years and 11 months, who seemed to have a speech problem. They didn't know what to do. They had also brought the child along and wanted me to talk to him as well, to understand the challenges they were facing.

As the counselling session progressed, I came to know the schedule of the child's daily activities. I was alarmed to hear that the child was spending about 4–6 hours every day watching cartoons on TV. When I tried to talk to the child, he spoke in a language which even I could not understand. After some time I came to realize that the child was speaking in a squeaky tone used by characters in cartoons and was trying to imitate them. As far as his hurried speech was concerned, it was due to the cartoons that he was watching as well as the volley of instructions from parents, who were always in a hurry and spoke very fast, even to the child.

I suggested to the parents to speak in a calm and composed manner to the child, giving one instruction at a time. The TV time needed to be reduced to 45 minutes and also monitored, that is, approved by the parents after going through the content. It took about three months for us to help the child unlearn the habit and speak in a normal manner.

Case 3

This is the case of Akash, aged 3 years and 9 months, whose mother was worried, because her son called himself Ram and did not allow anyone to call him by his name. He started behaving like Ram of Ramayan.

He had even started carrying a bow and arrow, which he had received on Dussehra day, almost everywhere he went. The other day he gave a shock to his mother by saying that just like Ram, he would also go in exile for 14 years.

Over a long talk, I came to know that the child had been introduced to Mahabharat and Ramayan in animated form, through CDs and television serials, which everybody in the family watched together. He also read stories of Ramayan and Mahabharat in illustrated books. Theirs was a joint family and all the family members were very religious. Thinking that these mythological stories were safe, they kept exposing the child to them over and over again, to such an extent that the child started relating to the character Ram. He made Ram his role model.

The mother was advised not to expose the child to Ramayan and Mahabharat in any form any more. She was asked to involve the child in other activities which were more appropriate for his age and gently wean him away from the concept of identifying himself with Ram. She was advised to clearly tell the child that such characters did not exist in reality. It was only after three months of constant efforts by the parents and the teachers that the child started responding to his name and no longer called himself Ram.

Children learn a lot through their environment because they are like sponges—they absorb everything they come across. So the work of significant adults like us is to take care of the environment which we are getting our children exposed to.

During their preschool years, children should not be given exposure to mythological TV serials and stories because they are not equipped to handle the difference between reality and fantasy, as their development is still not complete. Such is the impact of TV which many parents are not aware of.

Case 4

This is the case of Sehaj, aged 2 years 8 months. This child was becoming very aggressive. With each passing day, she would kick, hit, push, throw, and scream and always wanted to have her way. Her communication, too, was becoming aggressive and she started having problems at her preschool, when the mother came to me for a session of counselling.

While interacting with her in detail, I came to know that this child's preferred learning style was through movement but, unfortunately, she was not being taken for any outdoor activity, which was the required active play. So she had no choice but to watch TV, which was passive play for her. She was allowed to watch cartoons. The parents thought that this was the safest thing to do. However, the child required more movement than other children to use up the stored energy. Instead, her energy was hardly getting channelized. She was getting poor role models in the form of mental food to emulate and, unknowingly, she absorbed all the behaviour exhibited by the characters on the screen who were mostly hitting, pushing, kicking, and screaming.

The mother was advised not to subject the child to unmonitored TV viewing. Instead, she should get the child involved in active play by incorporating outdoor activities in the schedule of the child. This took at least three weeks to get implemented. Only then could we start seeing the results, both at home and at school.

9

Understanding the Looker, Listener, and Mover in Your Child

Have you ever wondered why your little one keeps you on your toes, always wandering and exploring the surroundings? Or why your child is always wanting to talk and is never tired of asking questions? Or why your child sits quietly and wants to wait for his or her turn, taking a long time in joining the group of children doing an activity?

Let us try to recollect how we learnt our lessons when we were studying. As far as I remember, I preferred reading a chapter aloud so that I could listen to the contents. Some of us may have moved around to learn, and some of us made our own acronyms and maps to memorize our lessons. Similarly, when we are attending a lecture or a presentation, we have different behaviour patterns. Some of us like the interaction, ask questions, and hear others speak. Some of us love the PPTs, the pictures, and videos. Some of us have to get up and walk around and wait for some experiential games to happen.

This is because all of us have our own preferred learning styles. Similarly, our little ones, too, have their own preferred learning styles. They fall in three categories—lookers, listeners, and movers, also called as visual learners, auditory learners, and kinesthetic learners.

So now, when you see that your child is always wanting to touch everything and explore the surroundings, rest assured that he or she is not being naughty but prefers to learn through movement. When your child talks ceaselessly, wants you to narrate poems and stories, and is never tired of talking and asking questions, please be sure that your child is learning through listening and talking. And when your child always wants to be the last to take his or her turn in a game, do not push the child because now you know that he or she is learning by observing others.

With this knowledge, when you observe your children, you will be able to recognize whether your child is a Mover, a Looker, or a Listener. Once you have the clarity as a parent, you need to handle their learning process accordingly.

Let us understand our Lookers, Movers, and Listeners.

Lookers: Children with this preference of learning style respond well when allowed to actually look at what is being presented, because they learn through images, they visualize things, and prefer to see a movie or read a book.

Movers: Children with this learning style need to be allowed to explore by touching, holding, and manipulating objects in order to learn. They are highly active and cannot sit for long. They have short attention span.

Listeners: Children with this preferred learning style benefit from hearing information. These children think in words, they verbalize concepts, enjoy using audio systems, and are musically inclined.

> *All of us have our own preferred learning styles. Similarly, our little ones, too, have their own preferred learning styles.*

Our aim, as involved parents, is to identify the preferred learning style of our children, identify their needs accordingly, and help and support them to build on the other learning styles as well. This is because, if children learn though all the three styles together, they will be able to maximize on all the learning opportunities available.

Let us look at some tried and tested strategies to build all the three learning styles in your children.

Proposed action plan to enhance Looker skills in Listeners and Movers:

1. Ask your child to call up relatives and friends by dialing and calling out loud the numbers to you. Children love this activity.

2. Allow your child to explore and express through brush and paints.
3. Get into the habit of going down the memory lane with the help of photo albums.
4. Prepare a "feely bag" where you put some items and let your child feel and recognize each of them.
5. Role plays are very helpful, where you can invent and act like real life characters. For example, your child can become the doctor and you the patient.
6. Fixing chart papers to cover the wall till your child's height will encourage drawing skills and hand-eye coordination. You can leave your child a picture message every day.

Proposed action plan to enhance Listener skills in Lookers and Movers:

1. Encourage your child to listen to sounds either through interaction with toys or CDs.
2. Engage in reading picture books together. Begin with one on animals. Children get fascinated by animal picture books. Talk about these books to your child.
3. Encourage role play. Children love to imitate one another as well as adults.
4. Keep hats, bags, toys, tools, and other accessories on hand and encourage both conversational and acting-out scenes.
5. Record your child reciting a poem and play it while enacting the same.

6. You can record your child's favourite story or rhyme, in your own voice, and put it as a background sound when the child is playing around so as to create an aptly stimulating environment.

Proposed action plan to encourage Mover skills in Lookers and Listeners.

1. Invest in a sandpit and let your child explore.
2. Make a paper stick by applying glue and rolling a chart paper. Tie a satin ribbon at one end. The child can play and dance with it, with background music.
3. In a bucket put balls, cars, plastic and metal toys, and some plastic tumblers. Let your child wash all the toys and give them a bath.
4. Go with your child on nature walks, "alphabet walks", leaf collection walks, and so on.
5. Dance and exercise with your child.
6. Take your child for outdoor activities every day.

Given below are some of my experiences as a counsellor:

Case 1

Karishma, aged 3 years and 2 months, was very shy. She did not want to try anything new or meet new people. The parents were very anxious and concerned and wanted the child to become an extrovert and a risk-taker. They wanted the child to develop leadership skills.

After talking to them at length, I came to know that the child's preferred learning style was through observation. Initially, the parents could not accept the fact, but slowly they started understanding the child better. They stopped comparing and pushing her. Instead, they started validating the emotions of the child. When the child did not want to come out to meet relatives or visitors, the parents would say, "It is OK. You can be in your room. In case you feel like meeting these people, you can join us later."

Since children at this age are great observers, they will observe and analyze before making a move. When not pushed, but hinted in a subtle way, they do what is expected out of them. There is nothing like shy children. These are children who are great observers and analyzers and take their own time to decide to act.

There was a marked improvement in the child, once the parents stopped being over-anxious and became relaxed.

Case 2

Kabeer, aged 4 years, was labelled as hyperactive and naughty by his parents and the teachers at school. The parents did not know how to handle the child.

After a detailed discussion, what came out was that the child's preferred learning style was through movement. He had a very short attention span. Not knowing this, the parents could not provide him with enough opportunities to channelize his energies. At school he was labelled as hyperactive, though actually he wanted to explore and learn. When he was forced to sit in one place, he would end up into a mode of movement, which was understood by the teachers as being naughty.

> Since children at this age are great observers, they will observe and analyze before making a move.

After the parents were made aware about his preferred learning style, they could understand the child's behaviour better. From then on, keeping in mind his needs, the parents provided an environment where he was allowed movement between tasks. The teachers started channelizing his energy by giving him tasks requiring movement. He was given the opportunity to explore and was no more called naughty. The child started improving because the significant adults understood him, his learning style, and his needs.

Case 3

Ananya, aged 3 years and 4 months, was frequently disturbing her teacher because she was always talking to someone or the other during class. The parents were really concerned because at home, too, she would want them to engage in a constant conversation. Her questions would never end.

During my detailed interaction with the parents, I came to understand the child was in the listeners or auditory category of learners. Therefore, there was this inbuilt need in her which urged her to talk and listen.

Once the parents understood her preferred learning style, they started providing her with opportunities which could take care of her needs. They gave enough opportunities for her to listen and talk. When the parents discussed this with the teacher at school, she, too, started understanding the needs of the child and gave her many opportunities to use her preferred learning style.

Case 4

The parents of Akanksha, aged 4 years, said that whenever they went out to any restaurant or anybody's house, the child would run to the washroom to check out the mirrors, the hand drying machine, and the liquid soap dispenser. She would want to touch everything. When they went to visit their friends or relatives, no matter how much they told the child to sit quietly, she would not stop herself from touching each and every thing which came in her way. Due to this, the parents were having a difficult time and felt embarrassed socially.

During the counselling session, I sensitized the parents to the fact that their daughter's preferred learning style was through movement and exploration. She came in the mover or kinesthetic category of learners, due to which she could not help touching and feeling things and wanted to know how to use them. So, when the parents felt she was restless and fidgety, she was actually not. She was simply interacting with the environment and trying to learn in her own way.

It was only when the parents fully understood, logically, as to why their daughter was always wanting to explore, touch, and feel everything, could they provide suitable opportunities to their daughter. They also stopped getting alarmed in social situations. Whenever they planned to go out, they could also prepare the child in advance about what was coming up and how she should go about it.

The A to Z of Parenting Today

After sending our children to a preschool, we want them to know their ABCs well. Here are some ABCs for you, as parents, and let us see how many alphabets you know!

A= Accept your child for what he or she is. Complete acceptance of the child is the key to building a healthy self-esteem in the child and a healthy parent-child relationship for life.

B= Believe in your child and have unconditional faith. When you believe in your child, the child automatically believes in himself or herself. Your faith and belief will propel your child to greater heights.

C= Connect with your child, as often as possible. Whenever your child calls you or has a question, attend to the child. Take that call because it might not come back ever again.

D= Discover your child's untapped potential by offering new experiences and new opportunities.

E= Empathize with your child and his or her emotions. Get down to your child's level to understand what he or she is going through. It is important to validate the emotions of your child, which means that when your child is hurt and crying, give him or her the permission to cry. You can say, "I know you are hurt and so it is OK to cry," whether your child is a boy or a girl.

F= Forgive the child and forget the past deeds, after deriving the learnings from the incident. Start afresh. Do not bring the mistakes of the past of your child to the present moment.

G= Give 100 per cent attention to your child every day, at least for 10–20 minutes. At that time, switch off your mobile, do not multitask, close your laptop. Be with your child completely at that moment. Ask your child to lead. You can also call this "me time" of the child, "me and mummy's time", and "me and papa's time".

H= Habituate your child to books. Nothing can be more beautiful than books. They are the best of counsellors, friends, and guides. Read to your child daily, spend meaningful time with books, take your child on a tour of the world through books.

I= Invest as much time as you can in your child. This will be your best investment, which will fetch you maximum returns for life, because you are your child's world.

J= Justify your actions and the instructions which you give to your child every day, by talking about the logic behind them. Do not try to get compliance by creating fear or by being an authoritarian parent.

K= Keep your promises—always. If you do not intend to fulfil your promise, do not make one, because if you fail to keep your promises, your child will stop trusting you and believing in you.

L= Listen to your child without being critical, judgmental, or a solution provider. Children just want to be heard, often without being interrupted.

M= Motivate your child by making regular deposits of genuine praise in the emotional bank. Do not forget to refill at regular intervals.

N= Never compare your child to another child—it is very detrimental for the self-esteem of your child.

O= Orient your child to be resilient. Be the right role model even in the worst of situations. Take every situation as an opportunity to learn and move ahead. Be optimistic.

P= Praise your child as often as you can. Try catching him or her doing positive things, instead of giving attention only when he or she does something wrong.

Q= Quantify your child's strengths rather than his or her weaknesses. This approach will ensure your child's healthy self-esteem for life.

R= Respond to your child's behaviour instead of reacting to it. The behaviour of your child is the result of something. Behind every behaviour, there are some emotional needs which you need to figure out as a parent.

S= Speak quality and not quantity. Always nagging the child will only make you a 24-hour radio channel. Your constant instructions might become only background music for your child.

T= Trust your child and respect him or her. This is the basic foundation of all relationships. Never jump to conclusions without first understanding the whole picture. Always trust your child.

U= Unconditionally love and support your child, especially when he or she least deserves love.

V= Value all the work of the child. Do not only look at the end product. Recognize all the efforts of the child. Remember, the process is more important than the end product.

W= Walk the talk. This means practice what you preach. If you tell your child that he or she cannot eat junk every day, you should practice it yourself for your talk to be effective.

X= Xpectation. Have realistic expectations from your children. Remember your child is from you, but not you. So please don't try to live your dreams through your child. It becomes too much for the child to handle.

Y= You are your child's world. You may be just another individual to the world, but you are everything to your child. So make yourself available to your child as often as possible.

Z= Zeal to learn and evolve as a parent should be your ambition. This will help you to remove your blinkers and broaden your horizon as an intuitive parent.

To conclude, I would like to say that you are blessed to be a parent. So make parenting your sacred duty.

All the best!

Wish you all a Happy and Informed Parenting!

Bibliography

Bharadia, Raksha, *Roots and Wings,* Rupa and Co., 2008.

Bloch, Douglas, M.A., with Jon Merritt, M.S., *The Power of Positive Talk,* Dolphin Press, 2005.

Bradway, Dr. Lauren and Barbara Albers Hill, *How to Maximize Your Child's Learning Ability,* Magna Publishing Co. Ltd., 1999.

Burke, Ray, Ph.D. and Ron Herron, *Common Sense Parenting,* Third Eye, an Imprint of Pentagon Press, 2005.

Cullinan, Bernice E., *Read to Me:,* Scholastic Inc., 1998.

Dutwin, David, Ph.D., *Unplug Your Kids,* Adams Media, 2009.

Faber, Adele and Elaine Mazlish, *How to Talk So Kids Will Listen and Listen So Kids Will Talk,* Perennial Currents, 2004.

Faber, Adele and Elaine Mazlish, *Sibling Without Rivalry,* Piccadilly Press, 1999.

Holt, John, *How Children Learn,* Da Capo Press, 1983.

Jain Hingad, Sugandha and Neera Jain, *Nurturing Emotional Intelligence,* Scholars Hub 2008.

Jain, Sugandha and Neera Jain, *Handling Behaviour Problems in Young Children,* Scholars Hub, 2006.

Kenny, Cedric M., *Love Without Spoiling, Discipline Without Nagging,* Wisdom Tree, 2004.

Prasad, Gitanjali, *The Great Indian Family,* Penguin Books Ltd., 2006.

Templar, Richard, *The Rules of Parenting,* Pearson Power, an Imprint of Pearson Education, 2008.